W9-CAY-749

CIRCLING FAITH

SOUTHERN WOMEN ON SPIRITUALITY

Circling Faith

The University of Alabama Press • Tuscaloosa

Edited by WENDY REED and JENNIFER HORNE

Typeface: Garamond Premiere Pro
Design by Michele Myatt Quinn

∞

The paper on which this book is printed meets the minimum requirements
of American National Standard for Information Sciences—Permanence of
Paper for Printed Library Materials, ANSI Z39.48-1984.

A complete listing of individual permissions can be found at the end
of this book.

Library of Congress Cataloging-in-Publication Data

Circling faith: Southern women on spirituality / edited by Wendy Reed
and Jennifer Horne.
    p. cm.
    ISBN 978-0-8173-1767-6 (trade cloth: alk. Paper)— 978-0-8173-
5701-6 (pbk.: alk. paper)—ISBN 978-0-8173-8608-5 (electronic)
    1. Southern women—Religious life. 2. Women authors—Religious life.
3. Spirituality. I. Reed, Wendy, 1966– II. Horne, Jennifer.
BL625.7.C57 2012
200.82'0975—dc23   2011034803

Cover: *Circling Faith,* 2011, by Bethanne Hill, www.bethannehill.com.

For my mother, Betty Reed

WENDY REED

For Julie and Jenny

JENNIFER HORNE

Contents

Acknowledgments

Thanks to the Alabama State Council on the Arts; the Seaside Institute for an Escape to Create fellowship; the Alabama Center for Public TV and Radio; Jennifer, the best coeditor and friend in the world; Dan Waterman; my friends; Greg, my copaddler; my Aunt Dianne; my mother Betty, and extra mothers, June and Anniece; my sisters, Jan and Brenda; my daughters, Brittany and Bri; and my son, Reed. And all the voices that keep the chorus of faith noisy.

—WR

Many thanks to my family and friends for your love and support. Thanks, also, to Dan Waterman at The University of Alabama Press for his patience and expertise and to Wendy Reed for riding the roller coaster together a second time. Finally, thanks to the readers of *All Out of Faith: Southern Women on Spirituality,* for their encouragement and enthusiasm, and for making me feel connected.

—JH

A Special Note on Barbara Robinette Moss (1954–2009)

DUANE DERAAD

Barbara was an artist and writer, but most of all she was a healer of hearts. She wrote this piece about a visit that occurred right after her first surgery. From that time until she died a little more than six years later, she published her second book, attended the Actor's Studio Drama School, wrote a screenplay that was a semifinalist at the Sundance Film Festival, wrote half of a book about her healing journey, pages of musings, rantings, poems, prayers, and encounters with doctors and healers. She also created more than one hundred pieces of art, had one-person art shows in New York City, Kansas City, Oklahoma City, and Des Moines, Iowa.

We were up many nights at 2:00 or 3:00 A.M. sitting with our fears and questions, the same ones she had asked Garret during that early visit. Often she would ask me if I thought she was going to live. During the later years I would have to answer honestly, "I don't know." Then we would review the reasons for hope, symptoms relieved, a little weight gain, two-mile evening walks. Then we would read poetry. Its beauty softened the fears and evaporated the questions. I always went back to bed thinking "that was really nice," in spite of the lack of sleep and knowing that I had to go to work the next morning.

Even though we always found reasons to hope, we also knew there was a very good chance healing would not come and we came to believe that whatever happened would be exactly what was supposed to happen. There was one exception to that acceptance. During the course of the six years, Barbara's fear of death, which initially was pretty intense, morphed into a fear of living with too much pain. The conversation on this topic always ended with, "If that happens, we will get on a plane for Oregon where assisted suicide is available, but we're not there yet." Strange as it may seem, this was a considerable comfort for her during the last two years.

Barbara died October 9, 2009, in the most peaceful, sacred place I have ever been. She did find healing, for herself, and for me. I learned that healing is not about delaying death, it is about how you live until you die, and how you die.

CIRCLING FAITH

Introduction

A Faith of Verbs

When our first book, *All Out of Faith,* was published in the fall of 2006, we didn't know what to expect from readers. The cover looked innocuous enough: dinner on the grounds framed with cross-stitching. Inside, though, the voices were anything but. We braced for controversy. Wondered how we would look tarred and feathered. Prepared our last words should we be roasted on a spit. In short, we were prepared to be attacked, reviled, criticized, and prayed over. It wasn't that the essays in the collection were heretical or blasphemous. They weren't. But they did something considered, by some, worse—they questioned. To have faith, after all, by one definition, is to accept without questioning. Isn't that what taking something on faith is?

Or is it?

Much to our surprise, as we traveled around to different conferences and bookstores and groups and talked to many different people, the book's upswelling of voices was welcomed. In fact, we found a community of like-minded spirits, not nearly as vocal or organized or visible as their traditionally religious counterparts, but strong in their conviction that no one could tell them what to believe just because they lived in the South. We might think of them as the spiritual descendants of Emily Dickinson, who wrote, "Some keep the Sabbath going to church; / I keep it staying at home."

Somewhat to our surprise, even the most devout appreciated the conversations that it initiated. And not just women. One man bought half a dozen books. He felt every woman in his life needed to know that her voice, no matter how different, counted. And that sort of counting had been a main goal for us. We'd said that if one person after reading *AOF* (we eventually acronymized the title) sends us an e-mail saying that she doesn't feel so alone, it will be worth all the work. That e-mail came the first week.

What also came were requests for even more voices. While we'd included a variety—Baptist Buddhists to preacher's wives to Jewish cantors—we discovered we'd only scratched the surface. People started cornering us in hallways. Tracking us down electronically. They wanted to volunteer. To share their experiences. To have their say. But they also wanted to read more. To know more. What did a tap-dancing astrophysicist have to say? Why not include an ordained Protestant minister who decided she needed to "leave church"? Where were voodoo and rock 'n' roll? Why leave out the Native Americans—again?

And so the idea for a second collection was born—not entirely planned, as is sometimes the case with birth, but nevertheless willingly conceived. "Should we?" became "We should."

With the new volume, although it is diverse and varied, we still sweated. Would the introduction be worthy of what followed, and would what followed be new and fresh? Would we be able to organize the essays into categories for the Contents? (*AOF* simply alphabetized, and like the voices, we wanted this one to be different.) And what would we title a book that covers sex, death, and blue jeans?

Loaded with such questions, we embarked on this second volume. The story begins: Two women and a laptop walk into a monastery. (There is no bar—the county's dry; there are no men—it's all nuns). For inspiration, they'd brought books. For sleep, they'd brought PJs. For thirst, they'd stashed a cooler in the trunk. This was before *Eat, Pray, Love* had sold millions of copies, inspiring women all over the world to seek spiritual retreat between periods of gelato and sex.

For over a hundred years, the Sacred Heart Monastery has been tended by Benedictine nuns. But it's struggling. Not many young women marry God anymore, the way a nun must. So they allow outsiders in. Even before *Eat, Pray, Love,* an individual could book a spiritual retreat for a nightly fee that included bed, breakfast, and dinner, simple fare made up partly of food from the previous meal. This was fine by us. We're not extravagant.

We stumbled into breakfast, the usual morning chitchat, when *Shhh!*—a nun shot us a look as we exclaimed over the hot table. What had we said that set her off? Seems like there was more shushing amid our wondering. At some point we understood—we were not allowed to speak until the blessing had been said, and the blessing wouldn't be said until the rest of the nuns had come in from their early morning prayers.

Unwittingly, we who had set out to raise the voices of Southern women were being asked to keep ours down, being placed under a very polite gag order.

We hadn't known the monastery's rules and were virgin diners in their cafeteria. "We're sorry," we apologized, because although the Benedictines herald from overseas, Sacred Heart was still in the Heart of Dixie and we were their guests. Southern guesthood comes with specially reserved towels, among other privileges, for the price of an unwritten protocol that includes following house rules, no matter whose house, even God's. So without asking a single question, we properly apologized and tiptoed off to sip coffee, to pray for bacon.

All this was before former President Jimmy Carter, who sees religion as one of the "basic causes of the violation of women's rights," spoke to the Parliament of the World's Religions saying, "Women are prevented from playing a full and equal role in many faiths, creating an environment in which violations against women are justified." This was before *The New York Times* touted the Dalai Lama as a feminist. Before a former faith healer, while eating a bowl of broccoli cheese soup, recounted how fire shot from his fingertips when under the influence of the Holy Spirit. This was pre-Obama. It was even pre-iPhone.

Of course, things would continue to change just as they had in the five years since the first book.

The more things change, though, the more they stay the same.

Women's numbers in the labor force increased, but only in the lower ranks. A year after the first book's publication, one poll revealed that the birth states of the two women with a laptop, Alabama and Arkansas, tied for first place in the nation with 75% who believe the Bible is literally true. Massachusetts and Vermont came in last with 22%. Apparently the faith gap between the North and the South mentioned in *AOF*'s Introduction wasn't shrinking. Southerners do possess an uncanny ability to believe in the supernatural, to have faith in the face of defeat. Some say it's what happens when Celtic and Cherokee mix. That the Scots-Irish have never privileged logic. Others say that the Scots-Irish never knew privilege, period. Historian Wayne Flynt says that in a region of an almost inhumane, hardscrabble poverty, it was the only thing they had.

With nothing to lose, staking everything on faith may not be so crazy after all.

In one sense, the first book had been an act of faith, and we, the coeditors, had to trust that it was something people would want to read, that the chosen voices could culminate with a chorus that was as harmonious as it was individual. We had held our breath, unsure of the coming reactions. One mother expressed delight to read of faith being discussed outside the church walls. For a while, she'd been telling people who asked, "We home-church."

Some two years later, we were driving to On the Brink, a literary conference in Jacksonville, Alabama. It was snowing in the Bible Belt. Parts of Alabama that never saw snow were seeing it pile up.

The question "What's keeping you alive?" had been raised, and this time we weren't under a gag order but a severe weather warning. The haze of white powder was foreign, but we had forty miles to go and the reception started in an hour.

We passed a pawn shop that proclaimed "Jesus Saves" right alongside "We Buy Guns." The oddest part, we decided, was that it didn't seem odd, and we agreed that it was a Southern thing, inexplicable to many, even—if we thought about it—to ourselves.

Not unlike faith, which often doesn't make sense, either.

It accepts stories about cutting off eyelids that sprout into tea plants and snakes that talk. It believes in holy cows, holy water, and holy ghosts. We know by definition that faith isn't sensible—it can't be tasted, smelled, touched, heard, or seen. It is defiant in that it defies the logic of proof. It is often religious, though not always. It incites and is insightful. It is blind but visionary. It is also an anchor, a rock that stands fast. It has even, with hope and love, been trinitized. It's been used over and over as a crutch and an excuse. And use is one measure that can stand the test of time.

The function of spirituality required some thought. And as we made our way, we deliberated the dailiness of faith, becoming increasingly curious, not about transformation as in the first book, but as a basis for staying open, for being malleable. Faith, we learned in the process of working on these two books, though we might wish otherwise, is not firm. Nor is it a settled state or a fixed noun. We've decided it is an ongoing process, a verb. We were sparked by a quote from Terry Tempest Williams: "This is my living faith, an active faith, a faith of verbs: to question, explore, experiment, experience, walk, run, dance, play, eat, love, learn, dare, taste, touch, smell, listen, argue, speak, write, read, draw, provoke, emote, scream, sin, repent, cry, kneel, pray, bow, rise, stand, look, laugh, cajole, create, confront, confound, walk back, walk forward, circle, hide, and seek."

So there we were, two women and a disco-only radio station, driving in what felt like a blizzard, throwing out verbs machine-gun-style: Damage. Wrench. Explain. Puzzle.

We were going to need categories for the Contents. But we found that partitioning faith, once we started trying, is nearly as impossible as defining it.

We resorted to brainstorming "-ing" words: Flummoxing. Annihilating. Undergirding. Fomenting. Hoping.

Although the snow was thick, it wasn't sticking and the interstate was surprisingly dry and seemed almost normal.

Reinventing. Re-upping. Metamorphosing. Rationing. Annotating. Transubstantiating.

By now it was getting dark and the snow had let up. But not us. We kept at it with a hell-bent, game show attitude, quitting only when we parked the car. With five minutes to spare, we made it to the reception with a category list that was more than promising and a thirst for copious amounts of red wine.

Voltaire said, "God is a comedian playing to an audience that is afraid to laugh." Are we afraid? Look around. See the group who won't drink caffeine, the group who drinks Kool-Aid. The ones covered by the blood of a Savior, the ones covered by burkas. The ones on their knees. The ones who won't eat pork. The ones who won't eat for days. We've looked and wondered. And the women who graciously grace the following pages wonder this and more.

What these writers discuss regarding faith does not distill its properties, or simplify its use and abuse. Their contributions pay tribute to its complexity. There is the wisdom of elders, the pull and intrigue of tradition, in Beth Ann Fennelly's, Marilou Awiakta's, and Brenda Marie Osbey's essays, and the knowing ways of embodying faith for Amy Blackmarr, Marshall Chapman, Barbara Brown Taylor, and Margaret Gibson. But knowing and knowledge, as Connie May Fowler, Alice Walker, Barbara Robinette Moss, and Cia White suggest, are not the same. Sometimes the navigation throws us off balance. Finding balance, according to Mary Karr, Debra Moffitt, and Susan Cushman, takes seeking. And seeking, Rheta Grimsley Johnson, Stella Suberman, and Mitzi Adams find, must occur amid multiple possibilities.

We appreciate each writer and her story. However, we are especially privileged to have some of the last words Barbara Robinette Moss wrote. Barbara died before this volume made it to print. So as she writes about being good enough to get into heaven, of being visited by her dead mother, of contemplating the essence of God, the shadow of her death while reading her essay is inescapable. The resonance of the essay's conclusion as she asks, "God, help me find my way," is haunting.

In reading and rereading these essays to see how to organize them and what to say about them, we found, strangely, that fully half of our new contributors had written either primarily or marginally about clothing, mixing the sartorial with the spiritual.

What did this mean?

We remembered wondering, as a child, why you had to dress up to go to church and being told that it had to do with showing respect to God, which included wearing a slip with your dress and, at first, gloves on your hands, a hat on your head. Was God some kind of fashion police? Did God listen only to those who were properly attired? Wasn't God more present in the exaltation you felt in the high limbs of a tree or in the feeling of running barefoot across a soft lawn, than in the itchy tights and hard patent-leather shoes you wore to church?

Of course, we do say *something* with what we wear: I want to be comfortable, I love the color red, I'd rather blend in than stand out, I feel sexy. It's all very well to consider the lilies in the field, but a lily never experienced closet trauma or wondered whether the field made her butt look big.

So maybe clothing is an apt metaphor for the "fit" of religious or spiritual practice. The wrong outfit can make you feel as though you are spiritually holding your stomach in. When you are wearing something that fits well and suits you, you feel unselfconscious, at ease. Clothing can also be changed; perhaps even worn in case of an accident.

As several of our essayists note, we are, after all, creatures of flesh *and* spirit. Remaining open to the wonder and mystery of both sometimes takes courage. With this book we are hoping to inspire conversation and encourage vulnerability, to challenge memory, to up the volume. What follows are voices, sartorial words echoing and tumbling, patching and mending, and perhaps, even in the end, redressing.

I

SEEKING

Faith in Motion and Stillness

Facing Altars

Poetry and Prayer

MARY KARR

To confess my unlikely Catholicism in *Poetry*—a journal founded in part on and for the godless, twentieth-century disillusionaries of J. Alfred Prufrock and his pals—feels like an act of perversion kinkier than any dildo-wielding dominatrix could manage on HBO's *Real Sex Extra*. I can't even blame it on my being a cradle Catholic, some brainwashed escapee of the pleated skirt and communion veil who—after a misspent youth and facing an Eleanor Rigby–like dotage— plodded back into the confession booth some rainy Saturday.

Not victim but volunteer, I converted in 1996 after a lifetime of undiluted agnosticism. Hearing about my baptism, a pal sent me a postcard that read, "Not you on the Pope's team. Say it ain't so!" Well, while probably not the late Pope's favorite Catholic (nor he my favorite pope), I took the blessing and ate the broken bread. And just as I continue to live in America and vote despite my revulsion for many U.S. policies, I continue to enjoy the sacraments despite my fervent aversion to certain doctrines. Call me a cafeteria Catholic if you like, but to that I'd say, Who isn't?

Perversely enough, the request for this confession showed up last winter during one of my lowest spiritual gullies. A blizzard's dive-bombing winds had kept all the bodegas locked for the second day running (thus depriving New Yorkers of newspapers and orange juice), and I found—in my otherwise bare mailbox— a letter asking me to write about my allegedly deep and abiding faith. That very morning, I'd confessed to my spiritual advisor that while I still believed in God, he had come to seem like Miles Davis, some nasty genius scowling out from under his hat, scornful of my mere being and on the verge of waving me off the stage for the crap job I was doing. The late William Matthews has a great line about Mingus, who "flurried" a musician from the stand by saying, "We've suffered a diminuendo in personnel." I felt doomed to be that diminuendo, an erasure mark that matched the erasure mark I saw in the grayed-out heavens.

Any attempt at prayer in this state is a slow spin on a hot spit, but poetry is still healing balm, partly because it's always helped me feel less alone, even in earliest childhood. Poets were my first priests, and poetry itself my first altar. It was a lot of other firsts, too, of course: first classroom/chat room/confessional. But it was most crucially the first source of awe for me, because it eased a nagging isolation: it was a line thrown to my drear-minded self from seemingly glorious Others.

From a very early age, when I read a poem, it was as if the poet's burning taper touched some charred filament in my rib cage to set me alight. Somehow—long before I'd published—that connection even extended from me outward. Lifting my face from the page, I often faced my fellow creatures with less dread. Maybe secreted in one of them was an ache or tenderness similar to the one I'd just eaten of. As that conduit into a community, poetry never failed me, even if the poet reaching me was some poor wretch even more abject than myself. Poetry never left me stranded, and as an atheist most of my life, I presumed its mojo was a highbrow, intellectual version of what religion did for those more gullible believers in my midst—dumb bunnies to a one, the faithful seemed to me, till I became one.

In the Texas oil town where I grew up, fierceness won fights, but I was thin-skinned—an unfashionably bookish kid whose brain wattage was sapped by a consuming inner life others didn't seem to bear the burden of. I just seemed to have more frames per second than other kids. Plus, early on, I twigged to the fact that my clan differed from our neighbors. Partly because of my family's entrenched atheism, kids weren't allowed to enter my yard—also since my artist mother was known to paint "nekked" women and guzzle vodka straight out of the bottle. She was seductive and mercurial and given to deep doldrums and mysterious vanishings, and I sought nothing so much as her favor. Poetry was my first lure. Even as a preschooler, I could sometimes draw her out of a sulk by reciting the works of e. e. cummings and A. A. Milne.

In my godless household, poems were the only prayers that got said—the closest thing to sacred speech at all. I remember Mother bringing me Eliot's poems from the library, and she not only swooned over them, she swooned over my swooning over them, which felt as close as she came to swooning over me. Even my large-breasted and socially adroit older sister *got* Eliot—though Lecia warned me off telling kids at school that I read that kind of stuff. At about age twelve, I remember sitting on our flowered bedspread reading him to Lecia while she primped for a date. *Read it again, the whole thing.* She was a fourteen-year-old leaning into the mirror with a Maybelline wand, saying, *Goddamn that's great* . . . Poetry was the family's religion. Beauty bonded us.

Church language works that way among believers, I would wager—whether prayer or hymn. Uttering the same noises in unison is part of what consolidates a congregation (along with shared rituals like baptisms and weddings, which are mostly words). Like poetry, prayer often begins in torment, until the intensity of language forges a shape worthy of both labels: "true" and "beautiful." (Only in my deepest prayers does language evaporate, and a wide and wordless silence takes over.) But if you're in a frame of mind dark enough to refuse prayer, nothing can ease the ache like a dark poem. Wrestling with gnarled or engrossing language may not bring peace per se, but it can occupy a brain pumping out bad news like ticker tape and thus bring you back to the alleged rationality associated with the human phylum.

So it was for me last winter—my most recent dark night of the soul—when my faith got sandblasted away for some weeks. Part of this was due to circumstances. Right after a move to New York, fortune delivered a triple whammy: my kid off to college, a live-in love ending volcanically, then medical maladies that kept me laid up for weeks alone. In a state of scalding hurt—sleepless and unable to conjure hope at some future prospects—suddenly (it felt sudden, as if a pall descended over me one day) God seemed vaporous as any perfume.

To kneel and pray in this state is almost physically painful. At best, it's like talking into a bucket. At worst, you feel like a chump, some heartsick fool still sending valentines to a cad. With my friends away for the holidays, poetry seemed my only solace for more than a month. Maybe a few times I dipped into the Psalms or the book of Job. But more often I bent over the "terrible sonnets" of Gerard Manley Hopkins to find shape for my desolation:

> I am gall, I am heartburn. God's most deep decree
> Bitter would have me taste: my taste was me;
> Bones built in me, flesh filled, blood brimmed the curse.
>
> Self yeast of spirit a dull dough sours. I see
> The lost are like this, and their scourge to be
> As I am mine, their sweating selves, but worse.[1]

I was also reading that bleak scribbler Bill Knott, to find a bitter companion to sip my own gall with. He'd aptly captured my spiritual state in "Brighton Rock by Graham Greene," where he imagines a sequel for Greene's book: the offspring that criminal sociopath Pinky Brown conceived in the body of pitiful Rose Wilson before he died becomes a teenager in a skiffle band called Brighton Rockers. This kid's inborn anguish resounds in the grotesque Mass his mom sits through:

Every Sunday now in church Rose slices

her ring-finger off, onto the collection-plate;
once the sextons have gathered enough
bodily parts from the congregation, enough

to add up to an entire being, the priest sub-
stitutes that entire being for the one
on the cross: they bring Him down in the name

of brown and rose and pink, sadness
and shame. His body, remade, is yelled at
and made to get a haircut, go to school,

study, to do each day like the rest
of us crawling through this igloo of hell
and laugh it up, show pain a good time,

and read Brighton Rock by Graham Greene.[2]

This winter, I felt yelled at by the world at large and God in particular. The rhythm of Knott's final sentence says it all—"to DO each DAY like the REST/ of us"—the first phrase is a stair plod, with an extra stumble step to line's end, where it becomes a cliff you fall off (no REST here)—"CRAWling through this IGloo of HELL."

People usually (always?) come to church as they do to prayer and poetry—through suffering and terror. Need and fear. In some Edenic past, our ancestors began to evolve hard-wiring that actually requires us (so I believe) to make a noise beautiful enough to lay on the altar of the Creator/Rain God/Fertility Queen. With both prayer and poetry, we use elegance to exalt, but we also beg and grieve and tremble. We suffer with prayer and poetry alike. Boy, do we suffer.

The faithless contenders for prayer's relief who sometimes ask me for help praying (still a comic notion) often say it seems hypocritical to turn to God only now during whatever crisis is forcing them toward it—kid with leukemia, say, husband lost in the World Trade Center. But no one I know has ever turned to God any other way. As the adage says, there are no atheists in foxholes (poet Stanley Moss says he was the exception). Maybe saints turn to God to exalt him. The rest of us tend to show up holding out a tin cup. Put the penny of your prayer in this slot and pull the handle—that's how I thought of it at first, and I think that's typical. The Catholic church I attended in Syracuse, New York (St. Lucy's), said it best on the banner stretched across its front: SINNERS WEL-COME.

That's how I came to prayer nearly fifteen years back, through what James Laughlin (via *Pilgrim's Progress*) used to call the "Slough of Despond," and over the years prayer led me to God, and God led me to church—a journey fueled by gradually accruing comforts and some massively freakish coincidences.

Okay, I couldn't stop drinking. I'd tried everything *but* prayer. And somebody suggested to me that I kneel every morning and ask God for help not picking up a cocktail, then kneel at night to say thanks. "But I don't believe in God," I said. Again Bill Knott came to mind:

People who get down
on their knees to me
are the answers to my prayers.
—*Credo*[3]

The very idea of prostrating myself brought up the old Marxist saw about religion being the opiate for the masses and congregations dumb as cows. God as Nazi? I wouldn't have it. My spiritual advisor at the time was an ex-heroin addict who radiated vigor. Janice had enough street cred for me to say to her, "Fuck that god. Any god who'd want people kneeling and sniveling—"

Janice cut me off. "You don't do it for God, you asshole," she said. She told me to try it like an experiment: pray for thirty days, and see if I stayed sober and my life got better.

Franz Wright states my position vis-à-vis my earliest prayers in "Request," here in its entirety:

Please love me
and I will play for you
this poem
upon the guitar
I myself made
out of cardboard and black threads
when I was ten years old.
Love me or else.
—*Request*[4]

I started kneeling to pray morning and night—spitefully at first, in a bitter pout. The truth is, I still fancied the idea that glugging down Jack Daniels would stay my turmoil, but doing so had resulted in my car hurtling into stuff. I had a baby to whom I had made many vows, and—whatever whiskey's virtues—it had gotten hard to maintain my initial argument that it made me a calmer mom to a colicky infant.

So I prayed—not with the misty-eyed glee I'd seen in *The Song of Bernadette*, nor with the butch conviction of Charlton Heston playing Moses in *The Ten Commandments*. I prayed with belligerence, at least once with a middle finger aimed at the light fixture—my own small unloaded bazooka pointed at the Almighty. I said, *Keep me sober,* in the morning. I said, *Thanks,* at night.

And I didn't get drunk (though before I started praying, I'd been bouncing on and off the wagon for a few years, with and without the help of others). This new sobriety seemed—to one who'd studied positivism and philosophy of science in college—a psychological payoff for the dumb process of getting on my knees twice a day to talk to myself. One MIT-trained scientist told me she prayed to her "sober self"—a palatable concept for this agnostic.

Poet Thomas Lux was somebody I saw a lot those days around Cambridge, since our babies were a year apart in age. One day after I'd been doing these perfunctory prayers for a while, I asked Lux—himself off the sauce for some years—if he'd ever prayed. He was barbecuing by a swimming pool for a gaggle of poets (Allen Grossman in a three-piece suit and watch fob was there that day, God love him). The scene comes back to me with Lux poking at meat splayed on the grill while I swirled my naked son around the swimming pool. Did he actually *pray*? I couldn't imagine it—Lux, that dismal sucker.

Ever taciturn, Lux told me: I say thanks.

For what? I wanted to know. Robert Hass's *Praise* was a cult favorite at that time, but despite its title the poems mostly dealt with failures in devotion to beauty or the disappointments endemic to both pleasure and marriage. Its epigraph had a man facing down a huge and ominous monster and saying—from futility and blind fear—"I think I shall praise it." Hass had been my teacher when he was writing those poems, and though he instilled in me reverence for poetry, his own pantheistic ardor for trees and birds mystified me. My once alcohol-soaked life had convinced me that everything was too much, and nothing was enough (it's a depressant drug, after all). In my twisted cosmology (not yet articulated to myself), the ominous monster Hass "praised" was God.

Back in Lux's pool, I honestly couldn't think of anything to be grateful for. I told him something like I was glad I still had all my limbs. That's what I mean about how my mind didn't take in reality before I began to pray. I couldn't register the privilege of holding my blond and ringleted boy, who chortled and bubbled and splashed on my lap.

It was a clear day, and Lux was standing in his Speedo suit at the barbecue turning sausages and chicken with one of those diabolical-looking forks. Say thanks for the sky, Lux said, say it to the floorboards. This isn't hard, Mare.

At some point, I also said to him, What kind of god would permit the Holocaust?

To which Lux said, You're not in the Holocaust.

In other words, what is the Holocaust my business?

No one ever had an odder guru than the uber-ironic Thomas Lux, but I started following his advice by mouthing rote thank-you's to the air, and, right off, I discovered something. There was an entire aspect to my life that I had been blind to—the small, good things that came in abundance. A religious friend once told me of his own faith, "I've memorized the bad news." Suddenly, the worldview to which I'd clung so desperately as realistic—we die, worms eat us, there is no God—was not so much realistic as the focal expression of my own grief-sodden inwardness. Like Hawthorne's reverend in "The Minister's Black Veil," I could only interpret the world through some form of grief or self-absorbed fear.

Not too long after this talk with Lux (in a time of crisis—the end of my marriage), someone gave me the prayer from St. Francis of Assisi. It's one of those rote prayers that cradle-Catholics can resent having drilled into them, but I started saying it with my five-year-old son every night:

> Lord, make me an instrument of Thy peace.
> Where there is hatred, let me sow love;
> where there is conflict, pardon;
> where there is doubt, faith;
> where there is despair, hope;
> where there is sadness, joy;
> where there is darkness, light.
>
> O Divine Master, ask that I not so much seek
> to be consoled as to console;
> to be understood as to understand;
> to be loved as to love.
>
> For it is in giving that we receive.
> It is in pardoning that we are pardoned,
> and it is in dying that we are reborn
> to eternal life.

Even for the blithely godless, these wishes are pretty easy to choke down. I mean, it's not hard to believe that, if you can become an instrument for love and pardon rather than wallowing in self-pity, then your life will improve. The only parts of the prayer I initially bridled against were the phrase "O Divine Master" and the last two lines about eternal life, which I thought were horseshit. Something of it bored into my thick head, though, for reciting it began to enact some powerful calm in me.

Within a year of starting the prayer, my son told me he wanted to go to church "to see if God's there"—perhaps the only reason that could have roused my lazy ass from the Sunday *Times*. Thus we embarked on what I called God-a-rama—a search entirely for my son's benefit; despite my consistent prayer life, I still had small use for organized religion. I ferried Dev to various temples and mosques and zendos (any place a friend would bring us) with no more curiosity than I brought to soccer (a sport I loathe) when he took that up. If anything, the Catholic church one pal took us to was repugnant, ideologically speaking. It set my feminist spikes prickling.

But the Church's carnality, which seemed crude at the outset—people lighting candles and talking to dolls—worked its voodoo on me. The very word *incarnation* derives from the Latin *in carne:* in meat. There is a *body* on the cross in my church. (Which made me think at first that the people worshipped the suffering, till my teenage son told me one day at Mass: "What else would get everybody's attention but something really grisly? It's like *Pulp Fiction*." In other words, we wouldn't have it any other way.)

Through the simple physical motions I followed during Mass (me, *following* something!), our bodies standing and sitting and kneeling in concert, I often felt my mind grow quiet, and my surface differences from others began to be obliterated. The poet William Matthews once noted that when his sons drew everyone as a stick figure, they evoked Shakespeare's "poor, bare, forked animal," which was—spiritually speaking—accurate:

they were powerless enough to know

the radical equality of human
souls, but too coddled to know they knew it.
They could only draw it, and they blamed

their limited techniques for the great truth
that they showed, that we're made in the image
of each other and don't know it.
—*The Generations*[5]

So the bovine exercises during Mass made me feel like part of a tribe, in a way, and the effect carried over in me even after church.

Poetry had worked the same way. I've written elsewhere of its Eucharistic qualities—something else Hass taught me. In memorizing the poems I loved, I "ate" them in a way. I breathed as the poet breathed to recite the words: someone else's suffering and passion enters your body to transform you, partly by joining you to others in a saving circle.

Prayer had been the first cornerstone. How could it not be? In language (poetry) I'd found a way out of myself—to my mother, then to a wider community (the poets I imagined for years), then to a poetry audience for which I wrote, then to the Lord, who (paradoxically) speaks most powerfully to me through quiet. People will think I'm nuts when I say I prayed about whether to take a job and end my marriage and switch my son's day care. I prayed about what to write and wrote a best-seller that dug me out of my single mom's financial hole. Of course, I also pray to write like Wallace Stevens and don't. I pray to be five-ten and remain five inches short. Doubt still plagues me. As Zola once noted vis-à-vis his trip back from Lourdes, he saw crutches and wheelchairs thrown out, but not artificial legs. Miłosz is more articulate about it in "Veni Creator":

I am only a man: I need visible signs.
I tire easily, building the stairway of abstraction.
Many a time I asked, you know it well, that the statue in church
lift its hand, only once, just once, for me.[6]

Prayer has yielded comfort and direction—all well and good. But imagine my horror when I began to have experiences of joy. For me, joy arrives in the body (where else would it find us?), yet doesn't originate there. Nature never drew me into joy as it does others, but my fellow creatures as the crown of creation often spark joy in me: kids on a Little League diamond in full summer—even idly tossing their mitts into the air; the visual burst of a painted Basquiat angel in Everlast boxing shorts at the Brooklyn Museum last week (can't stop thinking about it); my teenage son at night in the dead of winter burying our kitten in a shoebox so I wouldn't have to see her ruined by the car that hit her—his flushed face later breaking the news to me—a grief countered by my radical joy at his sudden maturity. In the right mind-set, the faces that come at me on the New York street are like Pound's apparitions, "petals on a wet, black bough." Inherent in joy is always a sense of *joining* with others (and/or God). The spirit I breathe in at such times (inspiration) always moves through others.

But nothing can maim a poet's practice like joy. As Henri de Montherlant says, "Happiness writes white." What poet—in this century or any other—has founded her work on happiness? We can all drum up a few happy poems here and there, but from Symbolism and the High Moderns forward, poetry has often spread the virus of morbidity. It's been shared comfort for the dispossessed. Yes, we have Whitman opening his arms to "the blab of the pave." We have James Wright breaking into blossom, but he has to step out of his body to do so. We have the revelatory moments of Tranströmer and the guilty pleasure and religious striving of Miłosz. W. H. Auden captured the ethos when he wrote, "The purpose of poetry is disenchantment." Poetry in the recent past hasn't allowed us much joy.

My own efforts to lighten my otherwise dour opus seem watered down. I thought of calling my latest collection of poems *Coathanger Bent Into Halo* (too clunky, I decided, but I was thinking how the wire hanger used for an illegal abortion could also be twisted into an angel's crown for a child's pageant). Still, the poems about Christ salted through the book spend way more time on crucifixion than resurrection. I've written elegies galore, love poems bitter as those of Catullus. I've written from scorched-earth terror and longing out the wazoo. My new aesthetic struggle is to accommodate joy as part of my literary enterprise, but I still tend to be a gloomy and serotonin-challenged bitch.

But doesn't dark poetry gather us together in a way that would meet the Holy Spirit's approval?

Rewind to last winter: my spiritual wasteland, when I received a request from *Poetry* to write about my faith. It was the third such request I'd gotten in a little more than a week, and it came from an editor I "owed" in some ways. How many times did Peter deny knowing Christ? I know, I know, my skeptical reader. It's only my naive, magical thinking that makes such a simple request (times three) seem like a tap on the shoulder from the Almighty, but for one whose experience of joy has come in middle age on the rent and tattered wings of disbelief, it suffices. Having devoted the first half of my life to the dark, I feel obliged to revere any pinpoint of light now. And writing this essay did fling open windows in me so the sun shone down again. I hit my knees, and felt God's sturdy presence, and knew it wasn't God who'd vanished in the first place.

Miłosz, who dubbed himself the "least normal person in Father Chomski's class," describes the sense of alert presence from prayer or the wisdom of age in "Late Ripeness"—a lit-up poem of the type I aspire to write:

Not soon, as late as the approach of my ninetieth year,

I felt a door opening in me and I entered

the clarity of early morning.

One after another my former lives were departing,

like ships, together with their sorrow.

And the countries, cities, gardens, the bays of seas

assigned to my brush came closer,

ready now to be described better than they were before.

I was not separated from people, grief and pity joined us.

We forget—I kept saying—that we are all children of the King.[7]

That's why I pray and poetize: to be able to see my brothers and sisters despite my own (often petty) agonies, to partake of the majesty that's every Judas's birthright.

Notes

1. Gerard Manley Hopkins, "I wake and feel the fell of dark, not day," *Gerard Manley Hopkins: Poems and Prose,* edited and with an introduction by W. H. Gardner (New York: Penguin Classics, 1985; reprint of 1953 edition).

2. Bill Knott, "Brighton Rock by Graham Greene," *Outremer* (Iowa City: University of Iowa Press [University of Iowa Poetry Prize]), 1989.

3. Bill Knott, "Credo," *Laugh At the End of the World: Collected Comic Poems 1969–1999,* Rochester, New York: Boa Editions, Ltd., 2000.

4. Franz Wright, "Request," *The Beforelife,* New York, New York: Knopf, 2002.

5. William Matthews, "The Generations," *Search Party: Collected Poems,* edited by Stanley Plumly and Sebastian Matthews, New York, New York: Mariner Books, 2005.

6. Czesław Miłosz, "Veni Creator," *Collected Poems, 1931–1987,* New York, New York: HarperCollins Publishers, 1988.

7. Czesław Miłosz, "Late Ripeness," *Collected Poems, 1931–1987,* New York, New York: HarperCollins Publishers, 1988.

Pilgrimage

DEBRA MOFFITT

I

The Mediterranean sun blisters Antibes's ocher cathedral and penetrates the worn stone steps. I tug at a thick wooden door and slip into the cool darkness away from the noise of the market and the high sea. Though I'm not Catholic, I've come here to weather the storm and marvel at Jesus. He stands in the shadows on a pedestal by a back bench and his heart holds a mystery. Though it is entwined in thorns, a flame leaps from it and his soft eyes glow. His outstretched hand urges me to start the journey. A tear falls.

I've been seeking for something spiritual since early childhood. Sitting on the wooden pew in the country church decades ago, I listened to the minister with wet underarms and sweaty forehead preach of inferno. My eyes drifted outside the screen window on that warm morning to the bee that lilted into the dogwoods and lilies. It followed an inner guide, drawn to sweet nectar. Mom tapped my arm to get my attention, but I swung my chubby legs and sniffled a protest about pinched feet. God required nice dresses according to her. So a lace bonnet, pastel yellow dress, and shiny black patent leather shoes replaced my usual jeans and sneakers.

In my tiny damp palm I held a paper heart we'd made in Sunday school. Now, my duty done, I ached to run outdoors through the fields and feel the warm caress of the wind. Oh, how I yearned to go. But this God of Sunday morning required sitting painfully still while the minister talked about how He would punish people who didn't go to our church, be baptized, and drink grape juice from tiny glasses that tinkled against the metal trays. "Be saved," he said and paused to let dread fill the air. His baritone voice boomed out and rose to crescendo. "For if you die on your way home, you will surely burn in hell for eternity." Even as a child I understood that fire hurt and tucked my heart deep into my pocket, away from the bleakness and fear.

When my body temple grew and turned me into an adolescent, I stepped forward. My sister and I had conspired a few days earlier to make our move. Not because we believed really, but because we felt parishioners nudge us with their gazes. Somewhere in the past weeks, our budding breasts brought on a change in our status and we realized we would be considered sinners until we took the plunge. By the time the minister reached the end of his lively descriptions of brimstone, we arrived nervously at the front pew to be baptized.

Embarrassed by outward displays of emotion even then, I hunkered into the pew, head down. "Do you confess your sins," he said. I nodded. My sister did, too. I was fourteen. In a splash we were behind the pulpit and submerged in the chilly baptismal font. It was a step ahead of my parents' days when the muddy river a few miles away served the same purpose. With a washcloth over my mouth, the minister dipped me back into the water until I was entirely submerged like a fish. As the water flowed out of my ears and my long dark hair dripped, I heard a chorus of voices rise to the ceiling, "Washes clean my sins."

As I grew into bigger, more practical shoes, the notion of God as one who takes vengeance and excludes ate at me. And was spiritual purity really as easy as a man bathing you with water? I've heard that if you take one step towards God, He will take ten towards you. So I began to ask questions and search. In the secret confines of my teenage bedroom decorated with beach posters and African violets, I read Gandhi, Zen Buddhist teachings of D. T. Suzuki, the Bhagavad-Gita, and Plato. I'd come from America, the land of choice. What if that preacher's God wasn't the right one for me? My God loves, I decided. I desperately wanted love. But where would I find it? As I turned eighteen, the desire to grow and know waned as preoccupations with a boy, college education, and a career increased.

Here in Antibes, crisis drives me back to the youthful yearning for something deep and meaningful. Before me in the cool shadows and blue-green of the stained glass windows, Jesus's burning heart welcomes the world to peer inside. Did the thorns of pain fan the flames that blaze golden and bright? Recently at work, I'd taken visitors to peer into the chest of a woman in the operating room at a clinic near Nice. By day, my less sensitive and poetic self marketed products for open heart bypass surgery. But my nights were filled with gory dreams when I learned that the job required taking doctors to see the products function.

The thought of seeing a human heart out in the air pumping under clinical eyes in the operating theater made me queasy. It was meant to be kept under wraps, hidden away and protected. But the doctor sawed open the rib cage and cauterized the folds of skin around the freshly opened wound of the woman whose face appeared waxen and lifeless. In a twist, he spread apart the ribs with a metal clamp and cut a thin whitish sack to reveal a fragile, pulsing, fist-shaped organ that must have survived many of the same life bruising shocks that I'd known. A hidden power surged through it as it throbbed in tune with the mysteries of the universe. In the concentrated silence, the doctor cupped it gently in his latex-gloved hand to prepare for intensive intervention. With a single electrical shock he stopped it and started the minuscule repairs.

I think of this now as I see Jesus's *coeur sacrée* in a human form and not the romanticized, cupidesque kind. I've been bypassing my own vital organ for many years, trying to survive on dry and arid reason alone. But when my body collapsed recently at Charles de Gaulle Airport, my French husband left, and my job vanished all at once, no amount of reason or logic could soothe the fear and anxiety that washed me over like a tsunami. "Everything will be fine," my head says. But even it doesn't believe this anymore. The loss of so much at once constitutes a *petit mort,* a little death, and demands a reevaluation. It seems to be exactly what I need to ask the right questions. Who am I? What's the purpose of life? I long for a miracle, for something real and enduring to heal me, provide answers, and fill the emptiness. Jesus's dark eyes remain knowing, silent. A still voice whispers, "Grow. Take the steps and grow."

II

At the Buddhist retreat, the lama from Tibet only promises the nature of mind—no heart. It's all about using breath for mental control. Perhaps if I learn to harness my mind, then the numbness will subside and I will feel my core again. I sit long hours on a mat in this grand white tent staked to the hills in the south of France and try to achieve equanimity. A chilly wind flaps through open spaces, and I keep my back close to the electric heaters. "Sit with your spine straight like a stack of gold coins," Rinpoche says with a Cambridge accent and laughs. He laughs a lot. When I ask about how to achieve illumination like the Buddha, he laughs again and hangs a white scarf around my neck to appease me. "It's all an illusion," he says. But the pain is real, I want to say, and feel confused.

"Sit with me," he says. The wind howls and a woman whispers excitedly,

"When the master says this, it's important. Pay attention. You'll get something out of it." I wait and watch, eyes half-open like the Bodhisattva, but without the peace. Nothing happens. My mind runs rampant across the room to a blue T-shirt like one my sister wore, to New York, where a friend takes the subway to work, to my comfortable sea view apartment in Antibes, where I can make an espresso coffee, eat dark chocolate croissants for breakfast, and watch the sun rise out of the sea. "Bring the mind home," Rinpoche says. I try to wrestle it back into this tent, but it continues to roam.

No comforts appear in this heaven. God here is the "Nature of Mind" and It expects hard mattresses, barren rooms (for those lucky enough to have rooms), a diet of legumes and milk. I don't mind this. Part of me adopts the monkish attitudes with joy. I would have been a good candidate for self-flagellation and hair shirts, too. In the afternoon we tend the flower beds and gather stones the size of soccer balls to build a wall around the garden. This is part of the work required during the retreat. How ironic. I'd come here to tear down walls, not build new ones. Later in line a scuffle breaks out as two aspirants dispute who will enter the cafeteria door first while rain batters down. Even at retreats egos battle for dominance and attention. I want to be first, too, but wouldn't it be better to let others pass ahead? We're all struggling with ourselves, taking steps along the journey. No one has arrived yet.

In the morning the lama asks if we prefer him dressed in his burgundy Tibetan robe or a business suit. The three hundred or so people mumble mixed replies. Later I meet him strolling on the road wearing a silk business jacket, as if spirituality is a business, too. The price we pay here would make it seem so. It's the first time I've seen him dressed like a Westerner. Yes, it's just a change of dress, just a role—and he is only human. I want and need something more— more substance, deeper explorations, someone who has drunk water from the well and can tell me if it is sweet. I'm grateful for his help, but still yearn for a power strong enough to tear the bonds from my heavy heart and heal it.

III

India's streets beat with the rhythm of Shiva's drums. He pounds out the dance of time with his feet, but in Mumbai and Bangalore, the dance is not a neat, tidy Western one. Here it is chaotic, vibrant, jostling, bustling life dancing its way through ravaged hearts. A plane takes me directly to the ashram. A place once reachable only by ox cart on dirt roads now has a small airport for dignitaries, foreigners, and anyone who can afford it. The face of the holy man appears on billboards, used by unscrupulous entrepreneurs to sell real estate, ayurvedic medicines, and incense. Monkeys clamber across the roads and eat the offerings of coconut, cucumber, and bananas from the shrines to Lakshmi and Ganesha. The gates to the city are painted cotton candy pink and baby blue. A free college and state-of-the-art hospital that specializes in cardiac surgery shine like jewels in the crown of this remote and parched South Indian land. I've heard that Gorbachev's visit here was followed by *perestroika*. This is a place for big transformation.

A three-wheeled motorized rickshaw with a statue of Krishna glued to the narrow dashboard takes me to the super specialty hospital. Not because I'm ill. I have a bad case of curiosity. I must see this ward where the holy man provides open heart surgery to anyone from any caste, religion, or country without discrimination and at no charge. A disgruntled doctor who worked there once said to the holy man, "Why should we provide care even to the rich who can pay?"

"When disease and suffering do not discriminate between the rich and poor, why should we?" he replied.

In America, this alone would be considered a miracle. Health care at no cost. The holy man provides it out of love, no strings attached.

The taxi drops me off in front of a pink and blue building that stretches a block long. From the outside it appears more like a Disney castle with rounded turrets. A long entrance with landscaped shrubs and green lawns contrast sharply with the arid, burnt, rocky backdrop of the hills. Signs line the path to the door.

"Love all, serve all." "Help ever, hurt never." I pass through the 12-foot-high doors into the marbled foyer replete with a hand-blown pink chandelier from Venice that was sent as a donation from a devotee.

In the corridor a small brown girl in a green gown walks past me with a huge smile and beaming eyes. The top of a scar peeks above her collar. If not for the generosity found here, she would have died. Her family could not have paid the price. Breathing the sacred air in this temple of healing, I silently ask for my heart to be repaired, too. A cool wind laced with incense blows through the halls; it carries reverence and devotion. Walking in the silence a subtle shift occurs, a thawing begins to replace the numb jadedness.

Later, back in the three-wheeled taxi, we course along the riverbanks, past a temple where a yogi performs "miracles" by making a coin appear and disappear. He materializes watches, too. But for me, no miracle compares to the giant hospital that provides free health care. In a world so focused on selfish ends, only a miracle of love could serve India's poorest—and the rich, too.

I sit cross-legged on the hard stone floors of the temple to see the benefactor firsthand. Dressed in a long simple orange robe, he performs *darshan;* he walks through the crowds of people from Azerbaijan, Qatar, Canada, Malaysia, Japan, China, Saudi Arabia, and America. Catholic priests sit in a place of honor on the veranda, next to Buddhist monks, Muslims, Hindus, Sikhs, and Christians. All come here on their search, attracted by this ocean of love. "Forms are many, God is One," the holy man says. "Go home a better Christian, if you are Christian, a better Muslim if you are Muslim."

Being a Westerner, the idea of a guru, a living teacher, conjures ideas of cults and loss of liberty. But here, in mystical India, where the psyche is laid bare under hot suns and monsoons, the teacher becomes a reflection of the better, higher, wiser, divine Self of the student. This appears in a dream. *I sit beside a path where a teacher dressed in a dhoti like Gandhi approaches. With my hands held together in prayer, I see him coming and wait for his benediction. I plan to bow down and touch his feet as the Indians do in a sign of reverence and respect. But when he arrives, he stops and bows to me instead. "Get up," I say, confused. "This is all wrong."*

"You are divine, too," he says.

A wave of energy washes over me when the holy man with thick black hair approaches. If I were less rational, I would say it emanates from him. "I am Love," he says. "I am God." I protest and feel shocked, but he speaks with a soft, sweet voice devoid of arrogance. But you, God? Is this a sign of ego? I smirk and take refuge in cynicism. Then he slashes away all my footing. "You are Love. You are God, too—only you have not yet realized it," he says, echoing the words of the teacher in my dream. I yearn for this to be my reality.

He speaks soothing words to a woman beside me who has cancer, and out of his palm comes a cross with Jesus and sacred ash. I find myself wiping away uncontrollable tears. Others weep, too. The suppressed hurts and sufferings that have accumulated in my body temple over these decades rise up into my throat and eyes and gush in streams down my cheeks, streaking my white cotton Punjabi dress. The shell around my heart melts away and the spark of light that I feared might be extinguished leaps into a bonfire, burning like the core of Jesus in the cathedral. In this precious moment of bliss, everything and everyone is love. We're caught up in a collective sea of love, tiny bubbles on the surface of the vast, deep blue, all connected. My heart leaps for joy and goes out to the teacher. I immediately grab it and put it back in its place. Not so fast, I want to say. But fragrant jasmine dances in on a light breeze and it's too late. I've become elevated and as subtle as the scent and oblivious to the bones of my bare ankles against the white marble floors. Nothing else in the world matters. Submerged in a tempest of sweetness, I stagger out into the bright sunlight and gasp for air. I love India, but I cannot stay here. If only I can take these lessons home and live them in my life.

IV

Having partaken of spiritual nourishment, now it's time to digest. I give away most of my possessions—the antique mahogany table, the 1880s map of Southern France, the gold jewelry from my ex—and move out of the Riviera apartment to a hermetic room in the Swiss Alps. Poverty and asceticism must be the way to enlightenment, I decide. My remaining friends and relatives look askance and let me go. I'm certain that if I spend long hours in silence meditating on God and fasting, I will understand and achieve liberation from my ego and merge. The extreme fervor I used in business now serves me in the spiritual realm. I intend to accomplish the goal now that I know what it is.

I spend long days in nature, hiking over Monte Cervello, along Lake Lugano, over rarely traveled trails and listening to the chorus of frogs. I see one huge frog lodged under a plate of glassy ice waiting to be released into the world when it thaws. Deeper and deeper inside I travel and listen to the silence. The lotus flower in my chest begins to expand, blossom, and flame, but it requires a controlled environment. In the winter the clouds enclose the view of the lake below and Ticino shivers under a blanket of white. This, I decide, is the time for the final cleansing. I will fast and be silent as a form of atonement until His birthday. This must be the path to illumination. Pulling the shutters to, I empty the fridge, finish my last supper, and leave a message on the answering machine that I will be away. A fresh *cachi* fruit and the last strawberries add to the heap of the compost pile as an offering to the garden gods.

In the darkness of the Alpine nights, the skies shimmer like velveteen fabric punctured with holes; the ethereal luminosity of the eternal sun shines through creating Pleiades, Orion, and Venus. I ignore my body wracked with hunger; my soul beats in tune with the core of the cosmos, in momentary peace and harmony, and spirals deeper into the mysteries of God.

The bells of St. Ambrogio chime on the ninth day, and on shaky legs I slip into the sanctuary of the twelfth-century church across from the house where a wide-eyed Jesus, nine hundred years old, emerges from the plaster. A man delicately removes the dust and paint that had covered him for centuries. He continues to work in silence with a brush while Jesus's ancient face is slowly made visible.

On the eighteenth day my shapely hips have nearly entirely disappeared and my pants require a belt to stay on. I am not my body. This is proof. The extra fat from my thighs dissolved into air; in the mirror my cheeks appear gaunt. I'm reminded of a skeleton painted on a Val Verzasca shrine to Mother Mary dating to the time of the plague. In Latin it taunted, "You are what I was. I am what you'll be." The skeleton acted as a not so gentle reminder of the nature of life. Generation. Organization. Destruction. GOD. Flesh comes and goes, but there's something more, deeper that is immortal.

On the twenty-first day, weak from taking only water, I prepare a hot bath and add a touch of myrrh. As I carefully enter into the ritual ablutions, I see my mind chatter as if its contents are nothing more than leaves floating down a river and I am the banks. "I want to go to a party," it says. "I'd rather be shopping at the Manor and eating at the Persiano restaurant." I watch and marvel at its ability to talk incessantly and identify myself with the observer instead of the mind. I am deep, fathomless, vast as the ocean.

Seeing this split is the reward for the sacrifice. For all of my life, I've considered I am my mind and limited myself to this. Now, I become the witness.

This moves me deeper into the inner labyrinth, but I have not yet realized the yearned-for climax of lights, bliss, and peace that knows no bounds. On the twenty-second day, I trek through the snow up to the *Vis à Vis* for Parmesan, olives, bread, and honey. This is my break-fast. In the aftermath, feeble and pale, I look back and shake my head. The flame in my heart is wavering because I did not get what *I* expected. Could it be that self-will is not the way? Extreme asceticism and retreat may have worked for saints, holy men and women in the past, but not for me. God has some other plan. In my ignorance I have yet to discover it.

V

Charlotte, North Carolina. I struggle with the forms. Jesus, the holy man, Buddha. "Forms are many, God is one," I hear repeated in my heart. In a dream during a rough night of fathomless diving and underworld pressure, I see Jesus. He smiles at me, his flaming heart visible, his face radiant. Buddha is there, too, and the holy man from India. They merge effortlessly into one. I struggle over this puzzle. Is it possible my heart is big enough to encompass them all?

After taking me to the South of France, Southern India, and Southern Switzerland, God has brought me to His South in the United States. I arrive hesitantly. Years of living like a monk in a remote Swiss village, enduring fasts and periods of silence to find God, do not prepare me for this divine joke. I hear Him laughing a big belly laugh like the lama; He never acts as I expect. "I just wanted to merge," I say. "Just let me fast myself into a silent oblivion." He gives me a man instead and sends me with him to Charlotte. After a vow of celibacy lasting many years and no desirable companion in view, I'd given Him a challenge. "If You want me to have a mate, then You'll just have to bring him here to find me." I lived in a village in the Swiss Alps perched over Lake Lugano. It contained seven hundred people, plenty of Swiss cows, goats, donkeys, chickens, and no single men. To anyone else this might have seemed unreasonable. But God can do anything. A few months later, Mike, a handsome man who grew up a mile from my parents' home in Indiana, showed up at my door. We had kissed once in high school and he reappeared in the Swiss Alps for a second date after calling Mom for my phone number.

I'd traveled across the globe, doing intensive spiritual practices for self-transformation, searching for love and understanding. This wasn't the answer I'd anticipated—marriage, a stepfamily, malls, renewed sexuality, megachurches, and getting my hands dirty practicing spiritual precepts in the material world. I doubted my direction. Had I taken a wrong turn somewhere? In times of deep need, answers often arrive through dreams that awaken me at 3 a.m. This one nudged me out of the silky dark night back into consciousness with a gentle breath of reassurance.

I walk outdoors, dressed in the white Punjabi I wore in India and in the Alps, where I felt serene. As I walk through the streets, they are ablaze with the radiant fire of Jesus's sacred heart. This is all I've been searching for. It's no longer closed off in a cage and set apart. It's no longer just one place in a cathedral, in an ashram in India, or on a mountain peak in Switzerland. It's no longer just inside of me, relegated to periods of silent renunciation. It's right here, now in the streets of Charlotte and on all roads leading everywhere. The holy man stands at the threshold of Belk's; Buddha joins the joy at the China Bistro and Jesus works out at the YMCA with his inner flame burning here just as it did in the cathedral in Antibes. People come and go in cars; their hearts glow, too, as part of this spiritual awakening—at the grocery store, in the post office, on the greenway. Jasmine vines around trellises sharing its sweet scent with good and bad alike. The maple shares its shade with all. All is One and nothing is set apart.

I've searched all over for something that is right here at home, but realizing it requires practice. It seemed easier to flee to India or sit alone in the serene Alps and fast. These were small tests. But in contact with people every day, my anger flares, my heart opens and closes. I am challenged to see God in my new husband, in his children, in the cashier at Borders, in the nurse who takes my blood and in myself. Love is, my dream says—when I have the eyes to see.

Chiaroscuro

Shimmer and Shadow

How a spiritual expat from the "Christ-haunted South" found healing through art and Eastern Orthodoxy

SUSAN CUSHMAN

Growing up in Jackson, Mississippi, in the 1950s and '60s, I was always attracted to powerful religious experiences. From my childhood years in the Presbyterian Church, through my involvement with religious movements on college campuses, and finally the Jesus freak hippies that formed a church in my first apartment, I finally landed within the walls of the ancient Orthodox Christian Church in the 1980s. It is no small thing to leave one's religious upbringing, especially in the South, for something as foreign as Eastern Orthodoxy. With this conversion came lots of changes, and the process continues today.

Head Coverings and Nuns

First I changed my name. I chose Mary of Egypt as my patron saint early in my conversion, changing my name from Susan to "Marye," and adding the "e" for

Egypt, a way of distinguishing her from Mary the Mother of God and other saints who shared her name. I began signing all my correspondence, "forgive me, Marye, the sinner," and naively used "sinfulmarye" as part of my original e-mail address. You can imagine the spam that hit my in-box.

My husband had become a priest in the Antiochian Orthodox Church, and so, to add to the peculiarity of my new nomenclature, I started using the Church's traditional title for a priest's wife—Khouriya—introducing myself in church circles and taking communion as Khouriya Marye.

Then I started covering my head in church. While head coverings are common in countries where Orthodoxy is indigenous, they're rare in America, especially in the South, even in our Orthodox churches. But the custom was cropping up in some convert parishes, and soon a half-dozen or so women at Memphis's Saint John Orthodox Church were covering their heads during worship. I'm sure my close friends and family were wondering where it would all lead.

And then I met the nuns.

Everything about Holy Dormition Monastery reflected a high level of care and attention to detail. The grounds were meticulously maintained, mostly by the nuns themselves, with some help from visitors. On one of my visits I asked if I could help clean the chapel. The nun assigned to the task showed me how to clean the iconostasis, the icons themselves, and some of the altarware used during services. We cleaned the windows, dusted the chairs, and lifted the oriental rugs to clean underneath them before laying them flat and vacuuming them, with special attention to straightening out the fringe on the ends.

"So, how often do you do such a thorough cleaning in here?" I asked, thinking this must have been a spring cleaning of sorts.

She looked at me as though she hadn't quite heard me. "Every Saturday."

The nuns didn't wait for the house of the Lord to get dirty before cleaning it. They kept it clean always, the way we should care for our souls.

The same nuns who had been busy cleaning and gardening and cooking and sewing vestments and painting icons and welcoming visitors during the day quickly found their way into the chapel at the sound of the wooden hammer rhythmically beating on the semantron—the gong-like instrument that called us to prayer—and the ringing of the bells before the evening service. When I entered the darkened nave, my eyes adjusted slowly to the candlelight, and my other senses came alive. All around was the sweet pungency of incense. As I took in the shimmering gold leaf of the icons, I realized the nuns were singing, beautiful Romanian melodies whose words I couldn't understand but whose sense I somehow felt. After asking a blessing from the abbess, the nuns took turns at the reader's stand. The ones who weren't chanting often prostrated themselves, rolling gracefully into little black balls on their knees for long periods of time, their faces to the floor.

The first time I heard them sing, I felt like Prince Vladimir's envoys to Hagia Sophia in Constantinople near the end of the tenth century must have felt. They had been sent to find a religion that Vladimir could embrace and offer to the people of Russia. After visiting the great cathedral, they reported, "We didn't know whether we were in Heaven or on earth." Although I had been Orthodox for six years before my first visit to a monastery, my experience of Orthodox worship up until then had been limited, for the most part, to my convert parish, which was still learning the ways of this ancient religion. The nuns at the monastery had grown up with the Orthodox faith—it flowed through them organically. They sounded like angels. Especially Mother Gabriella, whom I often refer to as simply "Mother."

I fell in love with Mother the first time I met her. This beautiful Romanian nun was about my age, and we had both married when we were only nineteen. But she married *Jesus*. Thirty years later she found herself serving as abbess of an active monastery that kept the traditional schedule of more than six hours of church services daily, while welcoming Orthodox clergy and hierarchs on a regular basis, serving dinner for up to a hundred guests most Sundays, maintaining a cemetery, a vegetable garden, a vestment-sewing business, an icon studio, and caring for visitors in its guest house year-round. In the midst of this busy schedule, Mother always took time to meet with her spiritual children from the outside world. She took me on; and, as I became a student of iconography in the monastery's classes taught by Russian iconographers, Mother Gabriella's guidance never wavered.

Painting Icons: Writing the Lives of the Saints in Colors

Iconography is spiritual work. It involves adherence to ancient canons regarding style, content, and even the choice of colors for the various subjects illustrated. After my first three workshops, I became frustrated with the harshness of the Russian instructors, so with Mother's blessing I traveled to numerous other places to study under iconographers from Greece and the United States. Eventually, I found my way back to the monastery to take a class under one of the Romanian nuns. For the next few years I explored a variety of these styles, always using egg tempera and gold leaf.

I painted dozens of icons over the next several years, and even began doing commissioned pieces, giving lectures on iconography, leading workshops at my church, and teaching classes in my studio at home. Iconography opened the door for me to find my way back to art—especially to writing. Or maybe I should say it was a way for me to come in the *back door* to art. As a spiritual discipline, it was looked upon favorably by the church and, more importantly, by my pastor and my husband, both of whom I still desperately wanted to please. It would be a few more years before I would take the next step towards self-realization as an artist. But first, I had more work to do on my wounded psyche.

Wisdom from a Spiritual Mother

It was the last day of my pilgrimage, and Mother had asked me to wait for her after lunch, on a bench under a tree that overlooked the vegetable garden. I always anticipated these talks with a mixture of anxiety and hope, as one might feel before a surgical procedure that held potential for great healing.

I sat on the bench, admiring the beauty of the sloping grounds, surrounded by deep woods which formed a protective border around the back of the monastery property. This was Michigan, and the pleasant breeze held none of the stifling heat of summers in the South. The Mother of God flower garden was in full bloom, and the vegetable garden was at its peak. As I waited for Mother to join me, I thought about what I would say to her this time . . . which struggles I would place in the light of her compassionate wisdom. She knew me well, having been my guide through various stages of my (ongoing) recovery from sexual abuse, eating disorders, and various addictive behaviors. She was always a safe place for me to land with my anger, especially when it was directed at the Church and its hierarchy. Yes, this spiritual home that I had found after my seventeen-year journey wasn't perfect. It was filled with broken people, just like me. But my experiences growing up with abuse and not finding safety even within the walls of the Church had left me in a messy and continuing battle with forgiveness.

Just as I was forming these thoughts for my talk with Mother, I noticed one of the nuns pulling weeds in the garden. This struck me as odd, because I knew they were excused from physical labor on Sundays, other than the necessary tasks of preparing meals and cleaning rooms in the guest house for incoming visitors. Bent over in her long black habit which covered every inch of her skin other than her face and hands, the nun labored meticulously, her works—and her very identity—hidden from the world's view. It was only when she turned and began walking up the hill towards the bench where I was sitting that I recognized her. Yes, the abbess of the monastery was pulling weeds in the vegetable garden. She approached me with a smile and sat beside me under the shade tree, placing the weeds on the ground at her feet to take care of later. I think she would have sat there silently for a long while if I hadn't hurried the conversation.

"So, how's your arthritis?"

"Thank God. It's not too bad today. Some of the sisters have had more pain with the cleanup work after last month's storm."

The day before I had seen an elderly nun driving a tractor, hauling broken tree limbs and other debris to the back of the property. I felt so bad for her that I offered to help, but after an hour or two, I was worn out and returned to the guest house to rest up for the evening's four-hour church service. But the old nun kept working right up until the bell rang for Vigil, when she climbed down from the tractor and headed into the chapel and approached the reader's stand for her shift as chanter.

"What's that?" Mother asked, pointing to the book in my lap that I had discovered in the monastery bookstore earlier in the week.

"It's Father Webber's new book, *The Steps of Transformation.* You know it?"

She nodded. "I think it does a good job of putting the Twelve Steps into an Orthodox framework. You finished or just starting?"

"Started it just since I've been here. It's . . . helpful. But, you know, as far as I've come in healing my lifelong wounds—through the sacraments and prayer and self-help books—it seems like I've still got an itch I can't quite scratch. I was wondering . . . do you think therapy would help?"

Mother was silent for a minute before speaking. She often did this, pausing to finger the knots in her prayer rope.

"It might, but the thing you have to be careful about with modern-day psychology is the temptation to think you can fix everything in this life. Some things might not get completely healed this side of Heaven. Maybe that itch is there to remind you that God's grace is perfected in our weakness. It's fine to seek healing, but we also have to learn to live with brokenness."

The Middle Way: Finding Balance

Mother had watched my spiritual metamorphosis from "Khouriya Marye" with my monastic yearnings for several years, back to "Susan," as I reclaimed my given name and focused my energies on finding balance.

After about five years of what some of my friends called my "nun phase," I took off my head covering and embraced my Southern roots. Manicures, makeup, and jewelry returned to my arsenal, and my long-neglected hair again received layered haircuts and blond highlights. The "new me" wasn't as glamorous as some of my Arab-American girlfriends, but I was making a move towards the center, and it began to feel good.

Soon after that visit I was asked to speak at a women's retreat hosted by an Orthodox parish in Austin, Texas. I chose as my topic, "The Middle Way: Finding Balance in Our Lives."

One of the talks I gave at the retreat was titled "Women Saints Who Found the Middle Way." Instead of recounting stories from the lives of saints who had lived in extreme poverty or who had experienced brutal martyrdoms while trying to preserve their virginity, I talked about married saints who served God in the everyday business of getting meals for their families, caring for the sick, and burying the dead. Rather than sharing the amazing but bizarre life of my own patron, Saint Mary of Egypt, I chose to speak of Saint Julianna the Merciful and Salome the Myrrhbearer, encouraging my listeners to find joy in living more conventional lives.

As John Maximovitch, the contemporary Russian Orthodox saint, said: "For all the 'mysticism' of our Orthodox Church that is found in the lives of the Saints and the writings of the Holy Fathers, the truly Orthodox person always has both feet on the ground, facing whatever situation is right in front of him. It is in accepting given situations, which requires a loving heart, that one encounters God."

So there I stood with this group of Orthodox women beside a river on a beautiful ranch just outside Austin, trying to keep my feet firmly planted. As I returned to Memphis, refreshed by my encounters with my new friends in Texas, I found another group of women waiting to guide the next steps of my journey.

Strong Women of Passion

In October of 2006 I attended the Southern Festival of Books at the Cook Convention Center, just a few minutes from my home in midtown Memphis. The program boasted a few of my favorite authors, especially Cassandra King, whose book, *The Sunday Wife,* had begun to soften the hard layers with which I had adorned my public persona. Meeting King, sharing my story with her, and having her write in my copy of her book, "To Susan, who knows what a Sunday wife is," were defining moments for me. I loved her even more after I read her essay, "The Making of a Preacher's Wife," in the first volume of *All Out of Faith: Southern Women on Spirituality.* She described her struggle—"balancing a Southern Belle, good-little-girl persona with that of an artsy wannabe who smoked cigarettes and dreamed of being a writer." And she wrote candidly about her years as a minister's wife, during which she "wrote devotionals and religious poems and church pageants, not out of devotion or true piety, but to please and impress others." Finally she "went underground" and wrote a novel about a preacher's wife who questions her life on many levels, stating that "the writing of it was my salvation."

As I listened to King and the other women on the panel for *All Out of Faith,* my heart was beating so loudly in my chest that I was afraid everyone in the room could hear it. On the inside flap of the book's cover, I read these words: "The South is often considered patriarchal, but as these writers show, Southern culture has always reserved a special place for strong women of passion." *That's me,* I thought. And in the Afterword, the book's editors, Jennifer Horne and Wendy Reed, wrote about how "spirituality is not removed from ordinary life but infuses it," and about the need to "go inside myself, below the roles I'd taken on as layers." *Yes.*

During the festival I also met Lee Smith, who was reading from her latest work, *On Agate Hill,* and the poet Beth Ann Fennelly, who paints a vivid picture of her own take on womanhood and spirituality in her poetry. She was reading from her latest book of poems, *Tender Hooks.* My favorite poem in that book is "Waiting for the Heart to Moderate," in which she describes what it feels like to be "all edges, on *tender hooks*" at every stage of a woman's life and to still feel the music "booming in her breastbone." I'm much older than Beth Ann, but I still hear that music, and like her, in my own efforts "to free it," I also worry that I "might do something stupid." But maybe my middle-aged heart is finally learning to moderate.

As the festival ended, I found myself thinking, *where have these women been all my life?* I hurried home with my autographed treasures and poured myself into the strong but tender female wisdom between the pages of their works. I rediscovered Sue Monk Kidd's writing, especially *The Dance of the Dissident Daughter.* And while my Orthodox embrace of the Mother of God differs from Kidd's approach to the "feminine imagery of the Divine," I benefited greatly from her wisdom concerning Favored Daughters who "carry the wound of feminine inferiority," trying to make up for it by setting "perfectionist standards. . . . A thin body, happy children, an impressive speech, and a perfectly written article."

Writing My Way to Wholeness

Or maybe a perfectly crafted *book*. Three short months after my encounter with these strong women of faith, I completed a novel. But it was a thinly veiled attempt at hiding my truth in the lives of the fictional characters I invented. And since I had an agenda, the characters weren't free to chase the creative rabbit trails they longed to pursue. So I laid them gently on a shelf (to be resurrected later) and I began to write my stories and submit them to literary journals and magazines. In just over a year I had seven personal essays published, so I strapped on my courage and began the work that had begged for an audience from the beginning—a memoir. A year later I realized I wasn't ready to go public with all aspects of my history, so I abandoned the memoir and returned to fiction. My current novel-in-progress features three strong women of passion as its protagonists. I don't know if the writing of it will be my salvation, but it is, at a minimum, an effort towards wholeness.

As the late Madeleine L'Engle said: "Until we have been healed, we do not know what wholeness is: the discipline of creation, be it to paint, compose, or write, is an effort towards wholeness. . . . The important thing is to remember that our gift, no matter what the size, is indeed something given us and which we must humbly serve, and in serving, learn more wholeness, be offered wondrous newness."

Learning to serve the gift through writing and painting is bringing wondrous newness into my life every day. Once it surfaced in an essay about how anger blocked me from painting icons, and how the beach, a dream, and a soft-rock pop song helped me get unblocked. At other times that newness has shown up to cheer me on as I embrace the darker aspects of my Mississippi childhood by laying down difficult chapters of my novel-in-progress. Sometimes I feel its presence during the sacrament of confession, when I've been up all night facing down my demons as I write, often chasing them with vodka or wine. Maybe my brokenness, like the egg yolks that I use to make tempera paint for my icons—themselves a form of life interrupted—is part of my offering to God.

II

KEEPING

Faith of Our Mothers

Taking *Terroir* on Faith

BETH ANN FENNELLY

I knew it was wrong, but I couldn't help myself. I was curious: too curious. I found myself stalking a website I'd bookmarked, one which promised "Discrete shipping on all orders." I placed the illicit item in my shopping cart, then took it out. I wanted to take one small step closer to full membership in my adopted home, my quest to be a Southerner. I wanted to eat dirt.

Not that dirt eating—also known as geophagy—is limited to the South, of course. The practice has been found on all continents, in various peoples, even in animals. And in all times: Apparently, people have been eating the earth since they've been walking the earth. Clays meant for consumption have been discovered at sites occupied by early humans. Historical references date as far back as Aristotle and Hippocrates of Kos (460–377 B.C.), who warned that "If a pregnant woman feels the desire to eat earth or charcoal and then eats them, the child will show signs of these things." Today, one can find women in Haiti drying mud cookies on their roofs. Clay eaters in Africa purchase their chosen variety in open-air markets and keep it in cloth belts, close at hand for snack attacks. In India, where Mahatma Gandhi advocated geophagia to cleanse the body, people have been known to drink tea from newly formed clay cups—and then eat the cups.

In the United States, geophagy has become associated with the South—usually with poor rural pregnant women, especially African American ones. Scholars such as Donald E. Vermeer and Dennis Frate call geophagy a "culture transfer" from Africa; slaves brought the habit with them to plantations, where it became known as *Cachexia Africana.* Plantation owners became concerned when slaves who ate too much clay became lethargic, and some owners went so far as to force their slaves to wear face masks to prevent them from geophagy. Yet while it is true that overindulging can indeed lead to anemia, intestinal blockages, and ruptured colons, Vermeer and Frate find it more likely that malnutrition, not geophagy, was responsible for the slaves' ill health. And despite the slave owners' vigilance, the practice remained, and spread to poor whites as well, as suggested by one of the nicknames for South Carolinians, "Sandlappers." My husband tells me his relations (poor white Alabamians) ate the clay mortar grouting the stones of the hearth at the family's home, the "Old Place"—weakening the structure until it threatened to collapse.

Geophagy's a dying tradition now. Due to the stigma attached, what remains has gone underground: Vermeer tells of the nurse in Holmes County, Mississippi, who pulled him aside one day to confess, "I just wanted you to know that I am also a practitioner." How much of the population shares her guilty habit is hard to determine; according to Susan Allport, author of "Women Who Eat Dirt" in *Gastronomica,* "In the 1970s, fifty percent of Black women admitted to eating clay, about four times the frequency among white women," but notes the percentage has since dropped. Vermeer hypothesizes that between thirty and fifty percent of pregnant African American women in the rural South consume clay.

That geophagy is a habit of indigent Southerners perhaps explains why it has such negative connotations. Geophagy is a subset of pica, a word which comes from the Latin for magpie, a bird known for its indiscriminate diet. The American Psychiatric Association defines pica as "Persistent eating of non-nutritive substances that is inappropriate to development level, occurs outside culturally sanctioned practice, and if observed during the course of another mental disorder, is sufficiently severe to warrant independent attention." No wonder the habit has gone underground, then; who would ask their doctor about its effects when Alexander Woywodt, M.D., can write starchily in 2002 in *The Journal of the Royal Society of Medicine* that "concealment of the aberrant eating behavior is an important issue. The diagnosis commonly emerges when a patient is accidentally discovered during a 'binge' of geophagia. Abdominal radiography can be of great help in the occasional patient who denies the habit."

Perhaps because there's no money to be made from advocating either for or against the eating of dirt, geophagy is ill-understood by the medical community. In fact, not only do doctors disagree about whether it's healthy or harmful, they disagree about why people do it. This much we do know: cravings are site-specific, which is to say, only a certain location yields the desired flavor and texture. The nineteenth-century Otomac tribe of South America preferred a fine red clay and would hike long distances to obtain it. North Carolinians, as historian Helda Hertz reported in her 1947 "Notes on Clay and Starch Eating Among Negroes in a Southern Urban Community," prefer "smooth, not gritty" white clay. The residents of Holmes County, Mississippi, prefer "hill dirt" to Delta dirt, and Frate tells of the popularity of a certain hill where he found cars lined up "like at a drive-in bank."

What's the dirt? We know that practitioners aren't running out into the garden to cram any old surface mulch in their mouths. It's pretty much the opposite of what Gabriel García Márquez describes in *One Hundred Years of Solitude,* where a woman in love "got up in the middle of the night and ate handfuls of earth in the garden with a suicidal drive, weeping with pain and fury, chewing tender earthworms and chipping her teeth on snail shells." Preferred clay is usually located in a band beneath ground level, and as such is uncontaminated with manure, parasites, or pesticides. Sometimes such a subsoil band will be exposed along a riverbed or, in contemporary times, through construction. Digging for clay in road banks has caused enough damage in some cases, according to Vermeer, to prompt the highway department to post signs requesting locals to stop digging.

While sometimes such clay is eaten right at the "dirt-hole," often it is stockpiled and baked into hard nuggets for gnawing, sometimes seasoned. Packages—with the clay's origin clearly marked—are sold even today across the South in convenience stores. Southern women who migrate North find themselves dirt-poor in a new way—and then send letters to relatives pleading for shipments. Luther Brown, Director of the Delta Center for Culture and Learning, says it may be apocryphal but he's heard "the post office in Anguilla was shipping huge volumes of clay up north." John B. Strait, geographer at Sam Houston State University, told me that he's tasted clay from Midnight, Mississippi, and Plains, Georgia, in Otha's Soul Food on Chicago's South side. "It wasn't bad," he e-mailed. "I had it with some vinegar and pepper, like one would eat with cucumbers." Geophagists who require their dirt come from a certain location are not unlike today's fashionable oenophiles who discuss "terroir," meaning the climate, soil type, and topography of a region that lend certain properties to a grape.

Is geophagy an illness or an affirming cultural practice? Experts disagree. Even *The New York Times* can only conclude, "Why hundreds of millions of people and dozens of animal species consume earth remains a mystery, and information about the health effects is contradictory and commonplace." Every expert I spoke to disagreed, but there are, to my count, five main theories.

The first theory is that pica satisfies hunger. Here we might look to the hero-ine of Pearl Buck's 1931 novel, *The Good Earth,* set during the reign of the last emperor of China, who serves her starving children "the good earth." There are similar historical cases—after a seventeenth-century famine in England, a Sax-ony official reported that "People finally started baking this earth and [. . .] the hill containing this white earth was undermined and collapsed killing five." But it's also true that geophagy exists in times of plenty.

A second theory suggests that people ingest earth to gain minerals lacking in their diets. This theory helps account for earth eating among pregnant women, whose nutritional needs are higher. Jared M. Diamond found that "Soils sold in Ghanaian markets to pregnant African women are richer in iron and copper than the dietary supplement pills made by pharmaceutical companies specifi-cally for prenatal use." Susan Allport notes that pregnant women in Africa often favor the clay of termite mounds which "are rich in both calcium and iron and supply a woman who eats at least twenty grams a day with more than 100% of her RDA for iron." The only problem with this tidy theory is that clays differ greatly in mineral quality and composition. In fact, for every pregnant woman who staves off anemia through clay, there might be a woman who induces ane-mia from clay, as clay can bind with iron molecules and prevent their absorp-tion.

A third theory argues that clay can neutralize poisons, especially in plants that have evolved toxins to prevent being eaten. This explains, perhaps, how the wild Andes potato became domesticated. The wild potato is toxic, but eth-nobotanists have seen Andes Indians dipping the potatoes in a slurry of wet clay (essentially mud) while eating them. As Allport writes, clays make effec-tive antitoxins because "their very fine particles give them a large surface area and make it likely that those particles will come into contact with the toxins in foods. And their crystalline structure is layered with positively charged ions, primarily of silicon and aluminum. Since many organic toxins are also positively charged particles, they essentially trade places with the ions in the clays, then pass harmlessly through the digestive system." Animals, also, can use clay to detoxify plants. In *Wild Health: Lessons in Natural Wellness from the Animal Kingdom,* Cindy Engel suggests that the scarlet macaws who eat clay from the Manu riverbed do so because their diet is high in toxic tree seeds, which the macaws detoxify by ingesting clay.

A fourth theory, and another that can account for pregnant women's cravings, is that it reduces nausea and indigestion. For years, the main ingredient in stomach-soothing Kaopectate was a white Georgia clay called kaolin. Formed millions of years ago of feldspar eroded from the Appalachians and carried by ancient rivers to the sea, these bands of kaolin are now covered by surface dirt. Kaolin has been found to reduce upset stomach and diarrhea, but it's valued more as an ingredient for high-quality glossy paper—it's what makes slick magazines slick. In *Red Clay, Pink Cadillacs, and White Gold: The Kaolin Chalk Wars,* the story of how mining companies tricked poor Georgia piedmont farmers into leasing away their mineral rights for a song, authors Charles Seabrook and Marcy Louza describe how "women in chalk country, like their mothers and grandmothers before them, still stroll occasionally down the back country roads, spoons in hand, to scoop chalk right out of the ground." But they also quote from a Macon physician who feels so strongly that eating clay can aggravate anemia that he goes on the radio to issue warnings.

Finally, scientists suggest that perhaps we eat dirt because dirt is good for us. *Why Dirt Is Good* by Mary Ruebush suggests that sheathing our children in mucousy layers of Purell is not only misguided but accounts for the rise in childhood asthma and allergies. Ruebush argues that when children eat dirt, they are allowing their immune systems to practice responding; in addition, dirt "plays a critical role in teaching the immature immune response what is best ignored." Could it be, then, that we are merely grown-up babies eating dirt out of an atavistic impulse which has survived because it gave us an evolutionary advantage?

One thing that the scientists rarely suggest as a reason for geophagy is an aspect I'm most interested in: taste. Which brings me to a sixth reason that people might eat dirt: they like it. Certainly that's what dirt eaters themselves indicate, who praise its pleasant sourness.

Having reviewed every theory, what is my takeaway? Where does all of this leave me in my quest to better understand my adopted South? No better off than when I started. Which puts me in the mind of, well, faith, to tell you the truth. I've been engaged in a similar, though more serious, quest to understand what I feel about religion for some time now. I was brought up Catholic—Irish Catholic, which is its own sect, or should be. I went to Catholic preschool, grade school, high school, and college. But I left the Catholic Church when I was twenty-one—not in a fit of adolescent rebellion, but after a sad and sober reckoning of my own deep internal conflicts with the Church's teachings—and I've been drifting ever since. Though in the past ten or so years, and especially since becoming a parent, I've felt that I need to better understand how I feel and what I believe.

I approach life's big decisions as a reader, because I believe we learn from the stories of others, that we educate our emotions by considering how different people at different times have faced the deep mystery of being human. But sometimes this philosophical stance falls short. Such has been the case with my decision to read about the major world religions and through reading decide which held the most promise. Even religious experts acknowledge the limitations of such a logical quest when they call for the "leap of faith"—there's a gap one must jump over, and following the bread crumbs of knowledge dropped in the forest by others before me can bring me closer but can't get me there.

And now I see that my interest in geophagy has mirrored the pattern of my interest in faith. The questions they present are similar. Both faith and geophagy are, for many, deepened by daily ritual. They are frequently site-specific. Like those scarlet macaws, we can find ourselves hungrier in some seasons than in others for their mysterious nourishment. Both tastes are often passed down, inherited from our parents. Both seem absurd to nonpractitioners.

Having rejected the land of my fathers and the religion of my fathers (and the absence of the maternal, in fact, is one reason why the faith of my youth ceased to fit) am I essentially cut off at the root? Can I make an intellectual decision to grow faith, or to crave dirt? Some people claim to be born with the desire to know God, the way some people claim to be born with the taste for clay. Is my lack of compulsion a disorder? A diagnosis? I find myself as an adult still feeling that Catholicism isn't right for me but feeling nevertheless a growing desire for something beyond myself. It's a vague but gnawing hunger, a hunger for a food I've never eaten yet. Somewhere out there must be the right religion; I just haven't found it yet. It seems strange to go church-shopping, but how else can I define and satisfy my needs? It seems strange to go dirt-shopping, but how else can I taste it, and therefore know if I like it?

I don't have access to the fireplace where my husband's Alabama ancestors dug their clay, yet I want to experience their South, at least as much of it as remains. So I found the next best thing to Alabama dirt: Georgia dirt. Late one night, I returned to the website I'd bookmarked, the one which promised "Discrete shipping on all orders." I placed the illicit item in my shopping cart. Confirm purchase? You betcha. "Home Grown Georgia White Dirt," kaolin from Toomsboro, was shipped UPS in a plain brown wrapper. Inside, the label on the zip-lock containing the large chalky nuggets read "Novelty Item: Not Intended for Human Consumption." Humbug. My teeth sank satisfactorily into a chunk. Like an iceberg calving, a small slab fell onto my tongue and I chewed it just a few times before it dissolved into a smooth paste. This two-stage texture was probably the best part—*mouth feel* is what food scientists call this—like gnawing on a solid chocolate Easter Bunny come August. Or, as my husband Tommy said, eating very stale Parmesan cheese. But the taste? Well, rather tasteless; chalky, with a strong finish of . . . chalk. I'd prefer the stale chocolate bunny. Or the stale Parmesan. Wondering if the hankering skips a generation, I handed a hunk to my four-year-old, who, um, didn't care for it. His tasting note: "Big fat butt dirt."

The search for a church has been a little more successful. My husband and I have been attending a service that doesn't feel so restrictive that we balk and chafe, but doesn't feel so loosey-goosey that we wonder why we bother to dress up. Yet I still wouldn't say I wake up on Sunday mornings with an urge to go there. And I certainly couldn't call it a compulsion. But I have the idea somehow that I should stick with it. Maybe the only way I'll learn whether I can nurture a craving is by feeding myself.

New research shows that, while in the uterus, fetuses and their mothers exchange stem cells. Of course we feel close to our offspring; we have become—at the cellular level—each other. And in many religions, we allow the body of another to become our own; the eating of bread, the symbol of a body, brings about rebirth. As for me, I took the body of the South into my body, and truth be told, I do not feel redeemed. But I'm sticking with it, at least for now. And I'm sticking with my Sunday services, too, though the dreamed-of clarity has not yet descended. So many others have found nourishment here. Maybe educating my palate is the first step. Maybe the leap comes next.

Amazons in Appalachia

MARILOU AWIAKTA

According to Albert Einstein, there is a dimension beyond time/space where time stands still—past, present, and future are one. My Cherokee ancestors knew how to enter this dimension at will. Since their spirits abide in my native mountains in East Tennessee, I walk with the strong, nurturing grandmothers that Timberlake met on his journey.

"Where are your women?"

The speaker is Attakullakulla, a Cherokee chief renowned for his shrewd and effective diplomacy. He has come to negotiate a treaty with the whites. Among his delegation are women "as famous in war as powerful in the Council." Their presence also has ceremonial significance: it is meant to show honor to the other delegation. But that delegation is composed of males only. To them the absence of their women is irrelevant, a trivial consideration.

To the Cherokee, however, reverence for women/Mother Earth/life/spirit is interconnected. Irreverence for one is likely to mean irreverence for all. Implicit in their chief's question, "Where are your women?" the Cherokee hear, "Where is your balance? What is your intent?" They see that the balance is absent and are wary of the white men's motives. They intuit the mentality of destruction.

I turn to my own time (1983). I look at the Congress, the Joint Chiefs of Staff, the Nuclear Regulatory Commission . . . at the hierarchies of my church, my university, my city, my children's school. "Where are your women?" I ask.

Wary and fearful, I call aside one of Attakullakulla's delegation. I choose her for the gray streak of experience in her hair, for her staunch hips, and for the lively light in her eyes that indicates an alert, indomitable spirit. "Grandmother, I need your courage. Sing to me about your life."

Her voice has the clear, honing timbre of the mountains.

I am Cherokee.

My people believe in the Spirit that unites all things.

I am woman. I am life force. My word has great value.

The man reveres me as he reveres Mother Earth and his own spirit.

The Beloved Woman is one of our principal chiefs. Through her the Spirit often speaks to the people. In the Great Council at the capital she is a powerful voice. Concerning the fate of hostages her word is absolute.

Women share in all of life. We lead sacred dances. In the Council we debate freely with men until an agreement is reached. When the nation considers war, we have a say, for we bear the warriors.

Sometimes I go into battle. I also plant and harvest.

I carry my own name and the name of my clan. If I accept a mate, he and our children take the name of our clan. If there is deep trouble between us, I am as free to tell him to go as he is to leave. Our children and our dwelling stay with me. As long as I am treated with dignity, I am steadfast.

I love and work and sing.

I listen to the Spirit.
In all things I speak my mind.
I walk without fear.
I am Cherokee.

I feel the Grandmother's power. She sings of harmony, not dominance. And her song rises from a culture that repeats the wise balance of nature: the gender capable of bearing life is not separated from the power to sustain it. *A simple principle. Yet, in spite—or perhaps because—of our vast progress in science and technology, the American culture where I live has not grasped this principle. In my county alone there are 2,600 men who refuse to pay child support, leaving their women and children with a hollow name, bereft of economic means and sometimes even of a safe dwelling. On the national level, the U.S. Constitution still does not include equal rights for women.*

The Grandmother can see this dimension of time/space as well as I—its imbalance, its irreverence, its sparse presence of women in positions of influence. And she can hear the brave women who sing for harmony and for transforming power. "My own voice is small, Grandmother, and I'm afraid. You live in a culture that believes in your song. How can you understand what women of my time have to cope with?"

Grasping my chin gently, the Grandmother turns my face back toward the treaty council. "Listen to Attakullakulla's question again. When he says, 'Where are your women?' look into the eyes of the white delegation and you will see what I saw."

On the surface, hardness—the hardness of mind split from spirit, the eyes of conquerors. Beyond the surface, stretching future decades deep, are crumpled treaties. Rich farms laid waste. And finally, the Cherokee, goaded by soldiers along a snowbound trail toward Oklahoma—a seemingly endless line of women, men, and children, wrapped in coats and blankets, their backs bowed against the cold. In the only gesture of disdain left to them, they refuse to look their captors in the face.

Putting my arms around the Grandmother, I lay my head on her shoulder. Through touch we exchange sorrow, despair that anything really changes. I'm ashamed that I've shown so little courage. She is sympathetic. But from the pressure of her arms I also feel the stern, beautiful power that flows from all the Grandmothers, as it flows from our mountains themselves. It says, "Dry your tears. Get up. Do for yourself or do without. Work for the day to come. Be joyful."

"Joyful, Grandmother?!" I draw away. "Sorrow, yes. Work, yes. We must work . . . up to the end. But such a hardness is bearing down on my people. Already soldiers are gathering. Snow has begun to fall. This time we will walk the Trail of Fire. With the power of the atom, they can make the *world's* people walk it. How can you speak of joy?"

"Because, for those who die, death is death. A Trail of Tears for the Cherokee, a Trail of Fire for all—it is the same. But without joy, there is no hope. Without hope, the People have no chance to survive. Women know how to keep hope alive . . . at least, *some* women do."

The reproach stings and angers me . . . because she is right. My joy, my hope *are* lost. I don't know how to find them again. Silently, my thoughts flow toward her. Hers flow back to me, strong, without anger.

"Come," she says.

"Where?"

"To Chota—the capital—to see the Beloved Woman."

I've heard of her—Nanyehi . . . "spirit person/immortal." Nanyehi, whom the whites call Nancy Ward and hold in great respect . . . the Beloved Woman whose advice and counsel are revered throughout the Cherokee nation. She is said to have a "queenly and commanding presence," as well as remarkable beauty, with skin the color and texture of the wild rose.

Not ready . . . I'm not ready for this. Following the Grandmother along the forest trail, I sometimes walk close, sometimes lag behind. Puny—that's what I am. Puny, puny, puny—the worst charge that can be leveled at any mountain woman, red or white. It carries pity, contempt, reproach. When we meet, the Beloved Woman will see straight into my spirit. I dread to feel the word in her look.

I know about her courage. She works ceaselessly for harmony with white settlers, interpreting the ways of each people to the other. From her uncle and mentor, Attakullakulla, she has learned diplomacy and the realities of power. She understands that the Cherokee ultimately will be outnumbered and that war will bring sure extinction. She counsels them to channel their energies from fighting into more effective government and better food production (she also introduces them to dairying). To avoid bloodshed, she often risks censure and misunderstanding to warn either side of an impending attack, then urges resolution by arbitration. In the councils she speaks powerfully on two major themes: "Work for peace. Do not sell your land."

All the while, she knows the odds . . .

As the Grandmother and I pass through my hometown of Oak Ridge, I look at the nest of nuclear reactors there and weigh the odds of survival—for all people. The odds are small. But not impossible. My own song for harmony and reverence with the atom is a small breath. But it may combine with others to make a warm and mighty wind, powerful enough to transform the hardness and cold into life. It is not impossible.

I walk closer to the Grandmother. In this timeless dimension, we could move more rapidly, but she paces my spirit, holding it to a thoughtful rhythm as we cross several ridges and go down into the Tellico Valley. We walk beside the quiet, swift waters of the Little Tennessee River. Chota is not far off.

What time/space will the Grandmother choose for me to meet the Beloved Woman? I imagine a collage of possibilities:

1775 Nanyehi fights beside her husband in a battle against the Creeks. When he is killed, she takes his rifle and leads the Cherokee to victory. Afterwards, warriors sing of her deeds at Chota and the women and men of the Great Council award her the high office she will hold for more than half a century. She is seventeen, the mother of a son and a daughter.

1776 Having captured the white woman, Mrs. Lydia Bean, Cherokee warriors tie her to the stake. Just as they light the fire, Nanyehi arrives on the scene, crying, "No woman will be burned at the stake while I am Beloved Woman!" Her word is absolute. Mrs. Bean goes free.

1781 At the Long Island Treaty Council, Nanyehi is the featured speaker. "Our cry is for peace; let it continue. . . . This peace must last forever. Let your women's sons be ours; our sons be yours. Let your women hear our words." (*Note:* No white women are present.)

Colonel William Christian responds to her. "Mother: We have listened well to your talk. . . . No man can hear it without being moved by it. . . . Our women shall hear your words. . . . We will not meddle with your people if they will be still and quiet at home and let us live in peace."[1]

Although the majority of Cherokee and whites hold the peace, violence and bloodshed continue among dissenting factions.

1785 The Hopewell Treaty Council convenes in South Carolina. Attending the Council are four commissioners appointed by Congress, thirty-six Chiefs, and about a thousand Cherokee delegates. Again, the Beloved Woman speaks eloquently. Knowing full well the pattern of strife that precedes this Council, she bases her talk on positive developments. "I take you by the hand in real friendship . . . I look on you and the red people as my children. Your having determined on peace is most pleasant to me, for I have seen much trouble during the late war. . . . We are now under the protection of Congress and shall have no more disturbance. The talk I have given you is from the young warriors I have raised in my town, as well as myself. They rejoice that we have peace, and hope the chain of friendship will never more be broken."[2]

Hope—that quality so necessary for survival. The Beloved Woman never loses hope. Perhaps I will learn the source of her strength by sharing her private moments: I may see her bend in joy over her newborn second daughter (fathered by the white trader Bryant Ward, to whom she is briefly married in the late 1750s) or hear her laugh among her grandchildren and the many orphans to whom she gives a home. Or, I may stand beside her in 1817 as she composes her last message to her people. Too ill at age seventy-nine to attend the Council, she sends the last message by her son. Twenty years before it begins, she sees the Trail of Tears loom ahead and her words have one theme: "My children, do not sell your land."

Nanyehi . . . Nancy Ward . . . "as famous in war as powerful in the Council."

The Grandmother's hand on my arm halts my imaginings. We stand at the edge of a secluded clearing, rimmed with tall pines. In the center is a large log house and around it women—many women—move through sun and shadow. Some walk in the clearing. Others cluster on the porch, talking quietly, or sit at the edge of the forest in meditation. Not far from us, a woman who is combing

another's hair leans forward to whisper and their laughter rises into the sough-
ing pines.

A great weaving is going on here, a deep bonding...

"This is the menstrual lodge," says the Grandmother. "When our power sign
is with us, we come here. It is a sacred time—a time for rest and meditation. No
one is allowed to disturb our harmony. No warrior may even cross our path. In
the menstrual lodge many things are known, many plans are made."

"And the Beloved Woman?"

"She is here."

"What year is this, Grandmother?"

"It is not a year; it is a *season*—you and the Beloved Woman are meeting
when each of you is in her forty-seventh season." From the expression on my
face, the Grandmother knows I appreciate the wisdom of her choice. Four and
seven are the sacred numbers of the Cherokee, four symbolizing the balance of
the four directions. It is the season when no women should or can afford to be
"puny." The Grandmother nods. Motioning me to wait, she goes toward the
lodge, threading her way through the women with a smile of recognition here,
the touch of outstretched fingers there.

With my hands behind my hips, I lean against the stout, wiry-haired trunk
of a pine. Its resinous scent clears my mind. These women are not the Amazons of the Greek fable. While they are independent and self-defined, they do
not hate men and use them only at random for procreation. They do not el-
evate their daughters, or kill, cripple, or make servants of their sons. But did the
Greek patriarchs tell the truth? If Attakullakulla had asked them, "Where are
your women?" they would have answered with a shrug. I'm wary of Greeks bearing fables. Although there is little proof that they described the Amazons accurately, ample evidence suggests that they encountered—and resented—strong

women like my Grandmothers and characterized them as heinous in order to justify destroying them (a strategy modern patriarchs still use).

In any case, why should I bother with distant Greeks and their nebulous fables when I have the spirits of the Grandmothers, whose roots are struck deep in my native soil and whose strength is as tangible and tenacious as the amber-pitched pine at my back.

Like the husk of a seed, my Western education/conditioning splits and my spirit sends up a green shoot. With it comes a long-buried memory: I am twelve years old. Mother has told me that soon I will be capable of bearing life. "Think of it, Marilou. It's a sacred power, a great responsibility." I think . . . and wait for the power sign. It comes. Mother announces to my father, "Our little girl is a woman now. . . ." He smiles. "Well . . . mighty fine." In the evening we have a dinner in my honor. Steam from corn on the cob, fried chicken, green beans, and cornbread mindless in my mind with the private odor, warm and pungent, that Mother describes as "fresh" (the rural term for mammals in season). I feel wholesome, proud, in harmony with the natural order.

I am ready now to meet the Beloved Woman.

"What was it like," you ask, "to be in her presence?"

"Come. I will show you." It is midnight/June/the full moon. Behind a farmhouse near the Kentucky border, you and I walk barefoot through the coarse grass. Crickets and treefrogs are drowsy. Birds are quiet. And we are enveloped in a powerful, sweet odor that transforms the night. Too pungent to be honeysuckle. Too fecund for roses. It recalls a baby's breath just after nursing, along with the memory of something warm and private that lingers at the edge of the mind . . .

Sniffing the air, we seek the source—and find it. The cornfield in bloom. Row on row of sturdy stalks, with their tassels held up to the moon. Silently, in slow rhythm, we make our way into the field. The faint rustle of growing plants flows around and through us, until, when we stop by a tall stalk, there seems no division between flesh and green. We rub the smooth, sinewy leaves on our cheeks and touch a nubile ear, where each grain of pollen that falls from the tassel will make a kernel, strong and turgid with milk. Linking arms around the stalk, we lift our faces to the drifting pollen and breathe the spirit of the Corn Woman—the powerful, joyous, nurturing odor of one complete-in-herself.

"Where are your women?"
We are here.

Notes

1. Ilene J. Cornwell, "Nancy Ward," *Heroes of Tennessee* (Memphis: Memphis State University Press, 1979), 41.

2. Pat Alderman, *Nancy Ward* (Johnson City, Tennessee: The Overmountain Press, 1978), 69.

Why We Can't Talk to You About Voodoo

BRENDA MARIE OSBEY

We who are natives of this City and count ourselves among the Faithful cannot talk with you, the outsider, about Voodoo. And that is unfortunate. Because in this highly complex, deceptively simple set of principles, beliefs, and what-have-you, is much that could heal you of whatever it is in your life that needs healing. Could heal your whole life, probably. Because that's what it really is all about. Your whole life. Not you personally, of course, but how the wholeness anyone and everyone should have can be restored, can restore one to oneself. But the very fact that you come asking after it means that you will never possess it, at least not in this lifetime. And certainly not from anything you might learn here. And besides, we honestly cannot talk with you about it anyhow.

You, of course, will tell us about the books you have read and the research you have done. None of which have anything to do with us or our beliefs. We will smile sympathetically as we always do at such defenses, which we recognize as the pleas for belonging that they are. Or perhaps you are a modern-day Latin—by which we mean that you are descended not from our oppressors of past centuries, but from the same oppression wreaked throughout the islands and inlands of what is now called Latin America. In other words, a cousin of sorts. In which case you will go on about Santería, which you will not call by its name, Santería, but, in hushed tones, "the saints"—as if the pope might have his spies nearby. As if the pope's spies had nothing better to do than loll about eavesdropping over iced coffees in New Orleans. You will go on about it and about your "love of Africa"; but what we will notice is your affection for things *European*. And how you use that word "European" as an adjective for all that is good not only about our City but about yourselves. You drop it like a compliment, without warning. We notice that although you come from the "race-less, class-less" worlds just next door to us, you *will* go on, at length, about color and texture and shapes of skin and hair and lips and noses. We will note with not a little shame the specific physical transformations you have foisted upon yourselves and freely recommend to us. By the time you return to "the saints," in other words, we will have begun to wonder if the pope's spies might not be needing their coffees topped. (Perhaps, for the sake of good manners, we ought to invite them to join us at the club this evening to hear our favorite bassist and his new trio.) You will notice our attention waning and become defensive (in another age we would say—why not?—*hysterical*). You will attempt to lure us with comparisons. "The drums!"—your voice rising now—"Where are the drums?!" (*In Congo Square,* we might offer, *every Sunday for the last few centuries.*) But we have heard all this before and so will offer more coffee—water? rum? sweets perhaps? Anything to take the edge off your confusion. And shut the door on that endless yammering.

None of this, of course, will satisfy you. Still, we will do whatever we can to put you at ease. You are, after all, a not-too-distant relation, and we feel for your discomfort. In the end, however, we will tell you nothing you care to hear. You will leave perhaps a little triumphant. But in a matter of hours, perhaps a day or two, some *dis*-ease will come over you and you will seek us out again. You will be calmer but no less unhappy. And we are sorry, truly sorry, for your distress. But we cannot help. We really cannot talk to you about it. Perhaps you should, finally, go home.

And indeed, wouldn't that be the very best thing for you, all of you, no matter who you are and how distantly or not-so-distantly related you might prove? Wouldn't it be better all around if you just turned about and went back home? We, for our part, would be quite content to see you go. We would like to imagine you, from time to time, lodged in some place as completely your own as this is ours. Then perhaps we might visit you and show by example how one ought to behave when visiting people in their homes. For that, in the final analysis, is what this is all about. This City is our home. And you—no matter how long your stay—are and will always be supernumeraries on the City stage.

Tourist-visitors are of course fairly easily dealt with. They rent their rooms, eat and fill up on liquor, take a turn about Bourbon Street, and are, for the most part, content. Friends are a bit more trouble. Friends have done us the courtesy of reading up on us, reading, that is, all of the books that we long ago recognized for what they are. Books intended for visiting friends who want to read up on us. You we take into our private places. You stay in our homes and eat at our tables for the duration of your stay. You we must (somehow) entertain. Still, at some point you will depart. Until the next time. Worst of all, without a doubt, are the bulk of you. The Transplants. Those who have chosen, for love (of a man or woman, a house or a street or a particular view) or for money (cheap rent or mortgage, usually) to reside in New Orleans. And that is all you will ever do. You will spend your Good Money (How surprised we are that you'd imagine our minding your spending only your "bad money"); you will Pay Taxes (*Someone* has to); you will Support the Local Institutions (This we truly appreciate). And come away discontented and up in arms. Or as we say, *all*-up-in-arms. (Long live local language.) You are and will ever be a Resident of the City of New Orleans.

Our Old Folk will look at you and shake their heads. Street youth will take advantage of you casually, simply to pass the time on long summer afternoons. Cashiers will take extra long ringing up your purchases. Art and antiques dealers, realtors and undertakers will begin to purr before you even reach the blocks their establishments grace. They can smell you over and above the River and eau de tourist vomit and piss. They will have fine-tuned their inventories and already written checks to their debtors by the time you arrive. They look up and smile. Genuinely. *This* is what you call *Service*. Still, the point of all this, and which I seem to have gotten away from, is that we cannot talk to you, any of you and especially you, about Voodoo.

We cannot talk to you about Voodoo because it is a sin. Laugh if you must. But have you gotten any further thus far than the most general replies to your questions? And how long have you been at it now?

Well. Here are a few general things that I *can* tell you. Because we're kin of a sort, after all. And there's a chance you'll linger about even longer if I don't.

Firstly, there are no dolls in Voodoo. That's a gimmick borrowed from European witchcraft to cheat the real tourists. Tourists apparently develop certain youthful tendencies almost as soon as they become tourists and so are inherently attracted to doll play. This is apparently accompanied by something of a mean streak that causes them to enjoy sticking things in their dolls. And so voodoo dolls have been built into the local tourism trade. But I can assure you from way-back-when: there are not now and have never been any dolls in New Orleans Voodoo.

I can tell you also that there are no queens, priests, or priestesses in Voodoo. Anyone who claims to be one is lying. And anyone who claims to have consulted one—and that includes Zora Neale Hurston and her laughable tales of snakes and nudity and black cat bones—is either lying, was duped, or some unfortunate combination of the two. That terminology—queen, priest, priestess—was never part of our religion.

First of all, the religion here in New Orleans is entirely within the sphere of women, whom *we* call Mothers. Clearly, men cannot function in this capacity. They may well work as herbalists or other kinds of *traiteurs,* but lack the capacity for what is called Deep Work. Deep Work requires a cleanness which only women possess. Men can work with roots or may call themselves psychics— whatever that means—but they can never "read," do Deep Work, or otherwise function as Mothers.

The next thing, which is bound to cause great disappointment for many, is that there is no initiation. It should go without saying that you cannot become non-existent queens, priests, or priestesses in a tradition that offers no initiation. No, you cannot "join" the religion here in New Orleans. If there is no initiation, how then does one become *"a Mother"?* you ask in disbelief. It's quite simple really. You are born into a lineage of Mothers. At some point, an Ancestress, a Mother from your own line, appears to you in a dream or a vision and you are afflicted. You may seek guidance from the Mother, but that's about all. And unless you know the proper language, you can't even do that. But that's another topic altogether.

As there is no initiation, so, too, there is no public ritual. Nineteenth-century *Daily Picayune* articles about "camps of Voodoos" on St. John's Eve; the fictions of George Washington Cable; twentieth-century inventions of Hurston and Robert Tallant; and the speculations of modern-day anthropologists aside, the religion here has never included public ritual or anything resembling group worship. It is a basic principle of the faith that whatever ritual is required takes place between the Mother and the Seeker, the Seeker and Nature—or some other environment—and in seclusion.

This is probably a good time to mention that St. John's Eve has no significance in our tradition either. St. John's Eve, also called St. John's Night, is lifted entirely from Western Europe. Like many Western religious holidays, it combines Christian with older European pagan rites and superstitions. In Christian practice, the birth of St. John the Baptist is celebrated on the twenty-fourth of June. St. John's Day is celebrated in Christian churches across the Western world with the blessing of crops and farm animals, feasting, and ceremonial bonfires. The date of the saint's feast, however, coincides with the traditional observance of the summer solstice, or Midsummer's Eve. And in Europe's older pagan practice, the eve of the solstice was the night when witches and other evil beings were believed to roam the earth with abandon and so was considered the most opportune time for the casting of magic spells. But New Orleans Voodoo recognizes neither the saint's feast day nor the solstice, neither European pagan rites nor the casting of magic spells. And so St. John's Eve is not observed as a religious or other holiday in our religion. Do I really need to mention now that there's no bloodletting, animal sacrifice, or snake dancing?

The next and most unpleasant surprise for you, in all likelihood, is that nobody here is the least bit interested in Marie Laveau. That's a hard one, we know. Yes, she was indeed a historical figure, a real flesh-and-blood woman. You can go to the City Archives to read her death certificate and learn that she died of diarrhea. Not even dysentery. Just plain diarrhea. Not an uncommon occurrence for someone living to an advanced age in those days.

A hairdresser by trade, Laveau was the first in what is now a long line of opportunists who saw in the religion the beginnings of a thriving tourism trade which, plied just so, could prove a continued source of personal wealth and power. It goes without saying that her clientele was made up entirely of whites who, ignorant of the religion *as* religion, sought her out for her so-called magical powers. And though she certainly never achieved anything like real wealth, to this day her name does strike wonder and awe in the imaginations of song writers, storytellers, visiting schoolchildren, and the uncounted sightseers who still flock to mark their Xs on her tomb. Here on the native front, however, even those directly descended from her have never been heard to acknowledge her with anything like dignity or respect. *That's what comes,* the Old Folk say, from *playing with the Dead.*

What I see as the larger problem than our not talking with you about our religion is the fascination it holds for so many of you. And this, I think, stems from the many and peculiar prejudices of the colonial mind. For one thing, any public gathering of three or more enslaved or free black people signaled to colonial whites cause for alarm. Such gatherings could only mean rebellion or Voodoo. The impending overthrow of white power or the ritual summoning up of black power—either one amounts to pretty much the same thing. It explains, too, the well-documented fear of drums and drumming. With all our modern day fondness for such expressions as "all things being equal"—which, generally, they tend not to be—it is relatively easy to forget that colonial whites, by and large, believed in the inherent magical nature of black people. That is to say, they quite often believed that blacks, so far removed, as they saw it, from themselves in historical and social and technological reality, were *naturally possessed of magical properties in their very persons.* Any Frenchman or Spaniard coming on a group of Africans here in New Orleans sitting together in a circle, either with or without drums, "naturally" feared physical or some other form of ill will. *This,* contemporary black folk might caution, *is what comes from enslaving people.*

Combine such inbred white superstition and fear with the inability to distinguish among folklore, popular myth, and religion—or simply between folk and formal religion—and you have the makings for a popular narrative in which anything can be believed or stated with impunity.

In addition to the injunction against discussing the religion outside the Community of the Faithful, there is also the desire, especially of working-class black people striving to advance in an ostensibly open and progressive society, not to be seen as Backward or Old-Timey.

More important, however, than any of these, is the inability and often sheer refusal to recognize in black speech, dress, behavior, and mores, the play of metaphor and symbol. Nobody believes, for example, that wearing a cross or holy medal, or that blessing a home or a child or a dead body by sprinkling with holy water constitutes an act of magic or superstition. Wearing a gris-gris or chamy-bag, however, clearly must be exactly that: an act of magic or superstition.

There is the problem also of naming. In the white colonial imagination, any and all belief systems particular to Africans and people of African descent are assumed to fall into the category conveniently dubbed—*what else?*—"Black Magic." And such names as Voodoo and Obeah have historically been used interchangeably to describe and contain and marginalize black belief. Black people don't have religions, only cults, superstitions, folk beliefs, something dubious called "practices."

Even belief itself manages somehow to become distorted. And this is evident in the way outsiders use language in their efforts to, quite literally, get a grip on the subject of traditional black religion. "Do you really *believe* in Voodoo?" or, "But Voodoo doesn't really work unless you believe in it, right?" or, my two favorites: "Do people in New Orleans still practice Voodoo?" and "I don't believe in that Voodoo stuff, but I don't mess with it either." Consider for a moment the outcome of substituting the name of any other religion. Logic and syntax fail instantly. The very idea of any Western religion somehow working or not working? *Do you really* believe *in Judaism? Catholic doesn't really work unless you believe in it, right? Do people in New England still practice Congregational? I don't believe in that Methodist stuff, but I don't mess with it either.* But of course this has to do with both the presumption of blackness as an eternally outsider experience and of New Orleans as a backwater where dark deeds are almost certainly always afoot. Is it any surprise then that we cannot talk with you about our faith?

Long before Hollywood showed us images of African, Caribbean, and African American wall-eyed shuffling, shrinking, superstition, and assorted buffoonery, Christian missionaries and antislavery proponents were serving up images of black sorcery and savagery. A fair part of many white abolitionists' reasoning was that the end of slavery would bring an end to the black pagan rites at the heart of so much rebellion and blood-thirst. Looking back at accounts of West Indian slave rebellions, the Reverend William Shepherd penned more than one cautionary poem. Writing more than half a century later, and paying special attention to the role of Obeah in inciting slaves to violence, Shepherd reflected on the 1760 Jamaican insurrection in "The Negro Incantation":

Hail ! ye sacred horrors, hail !

. . . .

Hail ! spirits of the swarthy dead.
Who, flitting through the dreary shade
To rouse your sons to vengeance fell
Nightly raise the troublous yell.

Hail ! minister of ill, whose iron power
Pervades, resistless, earth, and sea, and air
Blest by thy influence, happy be the hour
When we with magic rites the white man's doom
prepare.

Thus Congo spake. . . .

By the end of the eighteenth century, the realities of the Haitian Revolution had already brought changes in slave laws across the Americas. The role of African sorcery in firing and sustaining the twelve-year struggle for the overthrow of slavery was repeatedly cited as the beginning of the end of white rule. Here in New Orleans, new laws were passed in 1804, 1806, and 1809 to prevent the immigration of free blacks from the Caribbean and Latin America and especially to curtail the activities of what had long been the largest free black population. Even so, between 1790 and 1810, the free black population here increased by as much as 10,000. And early in 1829, the year that Shepherd's "Negro Incantation" was published in London, a rebellion not fifty miles outside New Orleans drove home the reality of the impending "white man's doom." Suppressing black religion was the most obvious tactic to corral insurrection and white bloodshed. Even in their efforts to present a sympathetic view of black humanity, many white observers of the period cannot help but posit black religion in opposition to Christian belief.

But Voodoo is neither at odds with Western religion in general nor is it especially in tune with Catholicism. Black New Orleanians are predominantly Catholic because the French and Spanish colonists established the Catholic faith as the official religion of the Territory and supported its institution with the force of law. Because New Orleans Voodoo is not Yoruba based, it relies neither on the intercession of multiple lesser deities, nor requires that African deities be "masqued" in the guise of Catholic saints. New Orleans religion recognizes a somewhat distant but single deity. The few Catholic saints that *have* been absorbed into the religion function both in their own right and as the servants of the Ancestors. They form neither the core of our belief, nor the object of anything that might be called worship. Rather, they retain their unique identities and function primarily as servants and messengers of the Ancestors. It is the Ancestors who are the heart of the religion and true focus of our attention because of their proximity to us. They were themselves once not only human but are also our kin and thus intimately connected to and concerned for us. In death, they continue to be so.

Unlike Santería or Haitian Vodùn, New Orleans Voodoo is not syncretic. It is not a blending of African and European religious systems. Saint X, for example, does not "stand for" Elegua or Yemanja; Saint X is Saint X and simply works for the Ancestors. In this way, the religion retains its identity as the agent of our deliverance from illness, want, even captivity. But we can't talk to you about that.

Let me put it this way. Suppose I had been born of my same parents but somewhere far from New Orleans, another country perhaps. I'd have been born and reared and become naturally fluent and conversant in the language, history, culture, and social graces of that land. I might very well go to church or temple or services as a faithful follower of one of the local or national or regional religions. My immersion in the sights and sounds and ways of that place surely would contribute to my own history and personality. It would not, however, erase my ancestry. And my mother, being who she is, would be careful to point me in the direction of the faith of my forbears. Even if she didn't, though, my Ancestors would still be mine and I would be theirs. Whether I acknowledge that linkage or not does not alter the fact of it. My place of birth would be the accident or "happening." Which is to say, I could *happen to* have been born anyplace. I would not, however, *happen* to be descended from enslaved and free black people from New Orleans any more than I would *happen to be* my own mother's child.

Our Ancestors, who we are taught make up the very source of our being, will always know us no matter where in the world we are born, live, or die. It's that way with the Religion. I cannot opt out of this history. No one in my lineage is as modern as all that. And besides, the Old Folk tell us, the Ancestors have all of eternity to call us to them. They're in no hurry, although we might very well have reason to be.

I can say, too, that people sometimes confuse the capacity of culture to expand, to assimilate outside influences, and to grow into newer forms with the notion that everything is accessible and available to everyone at all times. That outsiders always eventually become insiders.

New Orleans has always had a fairly constant stream of Voodoo tourists and thrill seekers. And the last twenty years have witnessed heightened and renewed interest, including documentary films and graduate theses and dissertations. These new narratives are no less sensational and voyeuristic than their earlier models. In addition to emphasizing the supposedly magical nature of the religion, the more recent studies tend to celebrate rather than discredit the reputed sorcery, now often referred to not as sorcery or black magic directly but as *shamanism.* And this championing of the magical nature of New Orleans religion says as much about the disposition of the champions as the earlier warnings did about the alarmists.

Rejecting traditional Western religion and embracing instead its presumed opposite is one way to escape the confines of Western religious and social authority and acceptability. But it remains bound to the marginalized view of magic and dark, magical beings. One of the claims of European witchcraft is that naming the devil gives one mastery over him. Isn't it possible that there remains some element of the old colonial desire to contain—and so have mastery over—at least one proven source of black resistance?

At the heart of the desire—especially of young-ish whites—to embrace Voodoo in New Orleans is a longing for inclusion in something at once forbidden, magical, and compelling in its dramatic appeal. Denied entry into the mysteries of the faith by its basic principles, these would-be initiates and devotees patch together aspects of European superstition, witchcraft, and folk Christianity, with miscellaneous Caribbean "practices" into a kind of spiritual mish-mash that they are pretty much free to make up as they go along. The dramatic element is undeniable. The practitioners of these newly amalgamated rites and rituals quickly go on to starring roles in a kind of ongoing theatrical production of their own making.

The Mothers say that the fakers and defrauders of tourists really take nothing from the religion because the religion lives within. A thief is doomed merely to take with one hand and lose with the other and so profits nothing and nobody in the end. In other words, in the long run, things balance out.

Western religion promises to open to us the gates of heaven, revealing an afterworld far better than anything we now know. In the oft-quoted passage, the Apostle Paul writes: "Now faith is the substance of things hoped for, the evidence of things not seen. For by it the elders obtained a good report." The later passage that almost no one references, however, reads: "For they that say such things declare plainly that they seek a country. And truly, if they had been mindful of that country from whence they came out, they might have had opportunity to have returned. But now they desire a better country, that is, an heavenly: wherefore God is not ashamed to be called their God: for he hath prepared for them a city." And it is just such a country and just such a city that interests the adherents of my faith.

As I child, I was taught that in the Land of the Dead, all of my own family was waiting to welcome me. It didn't matter that I didn't know them before because they knew me and always had and would not fail to claim me. That's the thing about Death. Through it we are restored to our True People, our True Place, our True Home, our Ideal City. We are made whole. And that's the point.

There are really three kinds and realms of being: this Living, the Dead, the Yet-to-Be-Born. Throughout our lives, we continually seek wholeness and healing, restoration, the way to the Land of the Dead, the path to the City of the

Ancestors. Such is the Community of the Faithful. Whenever we sit or stand or dance or otherwise turn in the circle, we affirm that continuity and claim our place in it.

As long as people are willing to pay for magic potions and Lucky Number 7 candles, or participate in "ghost" tours and staged rituals, at least one branch of the tourism industry is bound to thrive. And if doll play, snake dancing, and St. John's Eve celebrations suggest something of liberation or a good time to you, then by all means, as the Old Folk would say, run on with it. Don't let me spoil it for you.

The Mothers are right when they say that *comme'ce* is one thing and religion another. Faith lives within, they tell us; the whole is in the balance. The Ancestors know their own. And as sure as a liar lives and eventually dies by her own tongue, I have yet to hear of a so-called Voodoo queen who did not end badly. But I really can't talk to you about that.

III

EMBODYING
Faith in the Flesh

Magic

AMY BLACKMARR

> God is alive, magic is afoot.
> —Leonard Cohen

Summer, a blazing hot afternoon in Oklahoma City. I've got my hair up in a French braid and I'm wearing the clothes I call my mental health outfit: mint green linen dress and sand-colored sandals, silver Navajo bracelet, light turquoise paisley scarf tied to my leather bag. I'm visiting artisans' booths at the Red Earth powwow, and I've paused over a glass case of beaded jewelry I can't walk away from. "Those earrings," I say to friends who have peeled away from a writer's conference to spend the day at the powwow with me.

They step over to look. "Pretty," they say dutifully.

The earrings are Cherokee, long crystal cylinders hung from palest pink and blue beads threaded together in a delicate weave. I sigh, I pine, I linger, but alas, I can't afford them. Finally, I move away.

"Aren't you going to buy those?" asks Frank, stopping me.

"I can't."

"But they were made for you."

"I know. But I don't have forty dollars and I don't know when I'll have forty dollars."

"I'll give you the money."

"No. I can't pay you back."

"You don't have to."

I shake my head emphatically. "I can't do that."

"Look," he says. "I have the money, you want the earrings. Accept the gift."

I let Frank buy the earrings.

I put them on right away. When I tipped my head, they just brushed the tops of my shoulders. They tinkled beside my ear, like tiny wind chimes. The sound took me out of time. I'd be chattering away, and then I'd turn my head and suddenly I'd be standing in a field out West somewhere, watching the grasses wave and feeling the breeze on my face.

I used to dream about those beads. One night, I dreamt I was standing in a tall house set alone on a flat, colorless landscape. I was looking through an upstairs window. In the distance I could see the earrings, transformed into a crystal castle, suspended and shimmering like clear birds in the sky, surrounded by light. Years later—it was summer—I read Teresa of Avila's *The Interior Castle.* "Our soul," she wrote, "is like a castle made of a diamond or clear crystal, in which there are many rooms."

For five years I lived in a tarpaper shack beside a tea-colored pond on my grandfather's farm in south Georgia. He'd dragged the old commissary from his lumberyard out to the country and set it down beside a dammed-up branch of the Willacoochee River. The shack was our fishing cabin.

I used to spend days hunting in the fields and down in the swamps, borrowing the history I found there for my stories. One winter, way back at the far end of my neighbor Gene's rye field where it met up with the pines, I found half an Indian knife. It was white flint, flat, an inch wide and two inches long, plain, serviceable, and very old. The break was clean; the knife had probably snapped in two when Gene drove over it with his tractor. I searched for the other half for weeks, but it was lost. Eventually, I forgot about it. Two years went by, and corn, rye, peanuts. Plowing, planting, growing, harvesting. Plowing, planting, growing, harvesting.

November. I went walking in that field. Picked up raw peanuts and ate them, gave some to my dog Max. Reached down to pull a piece of flint from a clod of dirt, the flint white, flat, smooth, cool to the touch. Took it back to the cabin and there it was: the other half of that Indian knife.

Shiva danced the world into being.

At an art fair in Kansas, where I used to live, I was watching an artist sketch portraits. Beside him was a battered cardboard box of pictures. I'd always liked faces in art, so I started flipping through them and found a charcoaled African child wearing pale yellow beads, bare shoulders, bone thin. The eyes held something: the vaguest hint of light.

"Who is this child?" I asked the artist. He was drawing a teenage girl who sat looking bored in a straight chair nearby.

He glanced at the drawing. "Oh, no one I know," he said. "I support the world's effort to feed starving children in Biafra and he came into my head one day and I drew him."

I looked at the picture again. "How much do you want for it?" I said.

He thought about it. "Twenty-five dollars?" he said.

I got out my wallet. "All I've got is twenty."

He shrugged and took the money. I handed him the picture because he'd forgotten to sign it.

I laid the picture in the passenger seat of my car, and all the way home, I couldn't stop looking at it. I took it straight to a frame shop. When I got it back, I hung it on the wall in my den. One day, a friend came over to visit. I went to make tea in the kitchen, and when I came back, she was standing in front of it with tears in her eyes. "Someone took great care here," she said.

"He danced it."

"What?"

"That artist danced that child into being."

Wonder, wrote Thomas Carlyle, is the basis of worship.

On my desk under my monitor are two sea stars, a palm-sized round rock, a perfect arrowhead, a seashell encrusted with petrified coral, a beach agate, and a tiny clay mud man holding an open book.

In my carved Honduran box I keep four ebony Masai elders in red robes, who surround a sandstone bowl of water. I found them in a Savannah store two decades ago. I was living at Pop's cabin then, scratching by even for grocery money. Still, I couldn't pass those elders by.

I found the Honduran box in a Mennonite gift shop one summer day. The carving, which covers nearly the whole box, is of a tropical town with white-washed houses and thatched roofs. A woman walks away down a road, holding a basket on her head. The scene was so real, I kept going back to look at it. But the box was expensive, and I couldn't afford to buy it.

Nine months later, I visited the shop again, expecting the box to be gone; but it wasn't. I'd been trying to pay off my credit card for months, but I still bought that box. Now, every time I look at it, I'm in Honduras.

Suzuki said that ordinary life itself is enlightenment. Maybe ordinary things are, too. They touch something inside me, something that feels emotions I don't have names for.

Land can do that to me. Some places, like Pop's pond where I used to live, or the Florida Gulf on a still day, or eighty acres in Kansas I almost bought once, they move me, move inside me somehow. Going there is like stepping into a cathedral. A calmness takes me. Standing in a brome field beside a draw, examining a brown stone worn smooth by water, I hear a solitary meadowlark calling from a fence post, and suddenly I absorb the place like sunlight. I don't think about it so much as that it's just in me, a clear space I can go back to and rest in on days when I can't put my feet on that ground. Whatever I do, wherever I go, the spirit of the place stays with me, quieting me, like an arm of the Great Comforter, in an embrace that enfolds completely.

It seems strange that the material world can soothe so deeply: that's a virtue I'd always reserved to God. But because I can't touch the face of God, I find the Honduran box, the sea stars, the Masai elders, the artist's dream of a starving child and hold them close to me. It's like leaving the light on in the house when I go out for a walk. Coming back in the dark, I see that light in the distance, a consolatory refuge at the center of my troubled uncertainty. I surround myself with the things I can see that reach the place in me that loves, that is open, that knows wonder and astonishment and joy, and remember that the whole world is God, when I open my eyes.

Going to Church

A Sartorial Odyssey

MARSHALL CHAPMAN

I am not a churchgoer. At least not on any regular basis. The last time I went to church was Easter Sunday 1998. I'd been out in the yard digging in the garden when, at about a quarter 'til eleven, I jumped up and decided I had to go to church right then and there. My husband, Chris, agreed to go with me, so off we went, not bothering to change clothes or anything because we didn't want to be late. I just grabbed one of his clean, white oxford cloth Brooks Brothers shirts and threw it on over my Spice Girls T-shirt, gray sweatpants with garden dirt still on the knees, and flip-flops—beautifully showcasing a recent pedicure, I might add. Chris was somewhat more presentable in dress shirt, ironed khakis, and loafers.

The few times Chris and I have gone to church here in Nashville was to St. Augustine's Chapel on the Vanderbilt University campus. St. Augustine's is more or less an Episcopal church and seems to suit us fine. Chris calls it "Our Lady of the Holy Misfits"—a fitting epithet, seeing as the priest is a woman (complete with a tattoo) and members of the congregation on any given Sunday look like they each just landed from a different planet. The church itself is a steep A-frame, and everything about the architecture screams "early '60s." It sits up on a narrow, tree-shaded lot, wedged like a spiritual mediator between the Kappa Alpha Theta house and the Tri-Delt house, which amuses me whenever I think about how the Thetas and Tri-Delts were always at each other's throats, going for the same girls during rush, the same rebounds in intramural basketball, the same homecoming queen crown . . . you name it. I know about this firsthand as I was a Kappa Alpha Theta during my tenure as a Vanderbilt student some thirty-odd years ago, and I've heard things haven't changed all that much. But what amazes me is this: I have absolutely no memory of St. Augustine's ever being on the Vanderbilt campus during my four years as a student. Yet there it was, not ten feet away from the Theta house. My mind was obviously focused on other things.

My very first memories of going to church are faint and sketchy, mainly because I was just a toddler living with my family in Enoree, South Carolina. I lived in Enoree from right after I was born in 1949 until the summer after I turned five, which is when we all moved up to Spartanburg.

Enoree is a cotton mill town nestled above the banks of the Enoree River in the southernmost corner of Spartanburg County. In 2003, the main mill was shut down and demolished. Over the years, the automation of textile machinery, the opening of nearby I-26, and the influx of new industry had caused people to drift away. By the time the mill shut down, the village had become a ghost town. It saddens me to go there now and remember the close-knit community I grew up in—so full of life with children and dogs running from yard to yard, women out hanging clothes to dry in the sun, men sitting on front porches in their undershirts having a smoke, and Fesser Smith, the old black man, riding by on his motor scooter. Sometimes Fesser would stop and hand out sticks of Juicy Fruit gum to us children as we played on the sidewalk. His laughter still plays like music in my mind.

My family and I went to church every Sunday. We would have gone to a Presbyterian church since my father came from a long line of serious Presbyterians, but Enoree didn't have one, so we went to the Enoree Methodist Church. Enoree only had three churches: the First Baptist Church, the Enoree Church of God, and our Enoree Methodist Church. Of course, out in the boonies beyond Enoree, there was a whole slew of churches, mostly Baptist. The Cedar Shoals Baptist Church, the Lanford Station Baptist Church, the Beaver Dam Baptist Church, the Cedar *Grove* Baptist Church, and on and on. You couldn't go very far in Enoree without running into a Baptist.

Dad once told me the Baptists weren't allowed to dance. Not even on Saturday night. And Mother once got called down by the Enoree Church of God for calling a square dance at a Halloween carnival over at the schoolhouse. So the Church of God must not have liked dancing either. The Methodists weren't as hard-line on the dancing issue, which is a good thing since everybody in my family loved to dance. Dad's all-time favorite song was "I Could've Danced All Night" from *My Fair Lady.* Some evenings, he and Mother would jitterbug around the hi-fi in the living room to Glenn Miller and his orchestra playing "In the Mood." Even now, I'll wake up and put on some early Elvis record like "All Shook Up" and just dance, dance, dance all over my house. It helps get the blood going.

I only vaguely remember the red-brick-with-white-trim Enoree Methodist Church standing on a steep hill just up the highway from our house. But I clearly remember Sunday mornings getting dressed up for church. My hair got pulled tight into two little braids—or two ponytails if we were running late—then secured with rubber bands and colored ribbons. I liked the ribbons. They were pretty and smooth to touch. Then my feet were strapped into little black patent leather shoes that were stiff and hurt to walk in. I'd hold my arms straight up in the air while someone slipped on a scratchy crinoline petticoat, followed by my cotton church dress with the smocked front. I'd try to stand still for an interminable amount of time while the sash was tied into a crisp bow in the back where I couldn't see anyhow so why bother? The dress, including the sash, had been starched and ironed to cardboard perfection. No swaddling clothes here. These clothes hurt! And there was no way to get comfortable, much less get religion, sitting on a hard wooden pew in such a get-up. Every time I tried to lean back and relax, the knot in the bow of the sash would dig into my lower back, leaving a red wrinkly mark. There was nothing left for a five-year-old to do but fidget.

Early on, I stayed in the nursery while my parents attended church, but after I turned five, I got to go with them to "big church," as we used to call the adult service. I have two memories of being in "big church" in Enoree: one was of Mary Alice Jones's mother's arm and the other, a bird.

Mary Alice Jones's mother was this real sweet lady. She always smiled and was nice to everybody, but I was scared of her because of her arm. Her left arm ended at her elbow. No forearm, no wrist, no hand, no nothing—just a nub right where the elbow should have been. I couldn't help staring at it. Mother told me that it was rude to stare, but I couldn't help it. I was amazed at what all she could do with just that nub that looked more like a flipper. She could turn pages in the hymnal like you wouldn't believe. I have no memory of the preacher, the choir, the collection plate . . . nothing. Just Mary Alice Jones's mother's arm.

Then there was that Sunday a bird somehow got trapped in the sanctuary. Everyone in the congregation tried to ignore it, but not me. I watched in fascination while the bird swooped down over our heads, then thumped against one of the windows as it tried to get back outside with the other birds. Then it flew back up into the rafters where it perched for a while before swooping back down again. I could tell it was frightened and wanted to be outside. And I empathized with that bird, as I, too, wanted to fly up into the trees where there was fresh air and sunshine and other birds. Better to fly than fidget.

After we moved to Spartanburg and started going to the First Presbyterian Church, the clothes situation didn't improve. In fact, it got worse. Especially with the onset of puberty. Girls my age couldn't wait to carry a pocketbook and start wearing make-up, stockings, brassieres, and high-heels. This was around 1963 before the advent of pantyhose, when women had *garter belts* to contend with. And wire brush rollers, and Dippity-doo, and Clearasil, and Noxzema, and Dorothy Grey deodorant cream . . . and just all this *stuff.* Now, I was a late bloomer to begin with, not to mention a tomboy who liked being outdoors. I couldn't understand why the girls my age would hang out at Hardee's after school and smoke cigarettes while waiting for Gil Walker or Rusty Kitchell to drive by reeking of English Leather. *Homework* was better than that. But heaven was riding like the wind bareback on a horse named Delight out at Pierce Acres. And hell was sitting stiffly on a hard pew in church trying to keep my knees together.

One winter when I was about ten, two missionaries—a husband and a wife— came to speak during the regular Sunday services at First Presbyterian. They had just been to Africa, and I was real interested in hearing what they had to say, even though he was the only one who got to speak. His name was Dr. Small and he was from Scotland. Our regular minister, Dr. Weersing, didn't preach that Sunday so we could hear what Dr. Small had to say. Dr. Weersing just sat up by the pulpit in his big carved wooden chair listening along with the rest of us while Dr. Small spoke of Africa.

Dr. Weersing was the closest thing to God I had ever known. He had an assuring, mellifluous voice and preached a good sermon. I didn't know how good until after he left and . . . well, I won't go there. Anyway, Dr. Small's report from the dark continent got me to thinking. So much so, that by the end of the service I was convinced I had to ask Dr. Weersing a question. I expressed this desire to my mother and she indulged me. Together we waited until the congregation had pretty much dispersed, then walked over to the church office. We were greeted by Mrs. Clark, the church secretary, who showed us to an adjacent chamber where Dr. Weersing was in the process of taking off the heavy black robe he wore for church. I was somewhat taken aback to see him in a dress shirt and tie. It made him look like a regular person. He smiled benevolently while Mother explained why we were there. My heart was pounding but I looked him right in the eye and said, "Dr. Weersing?"

"Yes, child."

"Well, you know the natives in Africa that Dr. Small was talking about?"

"Yes. Go on."

"Well, what about the natives that have never heard of Jesus, yet they are *good* people . . . does that mean they will go to hell when they die?"

Mother, bless her heart, was right there with me. I could feel it. She gave me a strange look of love mixed with just a smidgen of fear. Together we turned to face Dr. Weersing, waiting for his reply.

"Well," he said, "they're not good if . . ."

"But suppose they *are* good," I interrupted. This made Mother nervous. Her ten-year-old had just interrupted God.

"You have to understand, Marshall. If they don't know Jesus, then they *can't* be good."

I looked down at my feet. He either didn't understand or didn't want to, so there was no use in talking anymore. Case dismissed. I can't remember what was said after that. Mostly Mother making nice as we made our exit. I sat in silence as we drove by Happy Hollow Park on our way to Papoo and Nannie's for Sunday dinner. There was no way for me to articulate what had just happened. But in my ten-year-old heart, I knew Dr. Weersing had not spoken the truth; therefore, he could not be God. And if he wasn't God, then who was? . . . Elvis? I wouldn't find out for another thirty years.

The third Sunday of January 1989
Nashville, Tennessee

I am alone driving west along River Road. The weather is nasty. It is sleeting and ice is everywhere. Even though it is mid-morning, the world seems dark outside my '78 Volvo. But there is a flicker of hope burning inside my forty-year-old heart. For I am driving to church on the first Sunday of my new career as Mother Teresa.

Earlier that week, I'd been discharged from a treatment center in Arizona where I was bombarded with all sorts of new information on how to live my life, you know, one day at a time. Forty days before, I'd checked myself in for depression. Twenty years of living the high-octane lifestyle of rock and roll was beginning to take its toll. After three days in DOE (detox, observation, and evaluation), the report on my "Suggestions for Treatment" form read: "facilitate grief of father's death," "break down denial of multi-substance abuse," and . . . something else about sex that I can't seem to remember right now.

I drive carefully along the curvy and ice-covered River Road for I am on my way to church—for the first time in nearly twenty years. I'd heard there was a good service at the chapel on the grounds at Cumberland Heights, a treatment center located in the rolling countryside west of Nashville. The recommendation had come with: "If bullshit was the criteria for cleanliness, you could eat off the floor in that place." Sounded like my kind of place.

That morning, I had arisen earlier than usual. As I dressed for church, I had to dig deep in my closet to find my only remaining pair of high heels, clean pantyhose, and a Calvin Klein black skirt with fitted jacket that I'd only worn to funerals. I then bundled up in my good Michael Kors long coat, big cashmere scarf, and black cashmere gloves. The weather forecasters were reporting a single-digit wind chill factor.

It was with a sigh of relief that I turned off the treacherous River Road into the driveway leading to Cumberland Heights. As I pulled into the parking lot, I took in a long deep breath, then stepped out onto the icy pavement. The effort it took to walk without falling damned near snuffed out that flicker of hope that'd been burning so brightly in my heart only moments before. "Shit!" I called out as my high heels slipped on the ice.

Though I wept uncontrollably at times during the service, I decided I would go back the following week. Sunday rolled around with the sun shining brightly in a dazzling blue sky. As I began dressing for church, I started praying out loud: "God," I began, "I really want to go to church today, but I don't want to wear those clothes I wore last Sunday. I nearly broke my neck trying to walk across that icy parking lot in those high heels. God, I hate high heels. I want to feel *good* in the clothes I wear to church. If you are not pleased with what I choose to wear today, would you just give me some sort of sign so I'll know? Thank you, God. Amen."

That morning, I pulled on my Nikes, a pair of 100% cotton sweatpants, and a 100% cotton Hanes T-shirt underneath a favorite cashmere sweater. Then I wrapped up in my big coat which hung all the way down to my Nikes, completely covering the sweatpants. I figured the sweatpants could be my and God's little secret.

At Cumberland Heights, I walked with confidence across the parking lot in my full stride. Whenever I walk that way, my lungs just naturally fill with air and all is well with the world. Even though I was early, the chapel was already packed, with people starting to sit on the floor in the aisle. Fortunately, I spied a little space in a pew about halfway down on the left. I walked down there and stopped. The person sitting on the aisle looked up at me and smiled. Then everyone in the pew, as if on cue, started scrunching up together so I could sit down. "Thank you," I whispered to each one as I sidestepped in front of them, taking care not to step on any toes.

When finally I sat down, I closed my eyes to get my mind focused on God. This was my first time wearing sweatpants to church and I was a little self-conscious, taking care to keep my coat closed over my knees. "Just give me some kind of sign." I smiled as I thought back to my prayer earlier that morning.

The first thing I saw when I opened my eyes was an embroidered message on the front of a backwards-worn baseball cap on the head of an African American teen-aged boy sitting directly in front of me. The words—less than a foot and a half from my face—said "FUCK OFF OR DIE!" I quickly looked around to see if anyone else had witnessed this serendipitous moment. (They had not.) Then I closed my eyes. "God," I said to myself, "I love you. You are a trip! Thanks."

My life today has changed a lot since then . . . in so many wonderful ways that I can't begin to count my blessings, though sometimes I give it a shot. And, yes, I hardly ever go to church. But on the rare occasion I do, I don't feel any differently there than I do at home or in the grocery store. It's like the whole world has become my church. And every breath I take is a prayer.

What the Body Knows

BARBARA BROWN TAYLOR

Yesterday I cleaned my closet, refolding the clothes worth keeping and making a tall stack of those I no longer wear. Lots of souvenir T-shirts went into the castoff pile, along with any pair of pants that had more pleats than pockets. As usual, I granted an exception to the blue jean cutoffs I have not worn since my sophomore year in college.

For more than thirty years now, I have declined to part with them. Every time I hold them up, I can smell the fresh-mown grass on the quadrangle, where I lay with my boyfriend's head in my lap. I can hear the din in the dining hall, where I bent over too many plates of macaroni and cheese with my vegetarian friends. The gray spots on the back pocket date to a Vietnam era production of *The Serpent* by Jean-Claude van Itallie, for which I painted scenery and learned the lines of the Fourth Woman.

After the Third Woman said, "I'm in the middle," I rose up out of the writhing mass of bodies on the stage and said, "Knowing neither the end nor the beginning." It was a prescient thing for a nineteen-year-old to say, even if someone else wrote it for me. During that same year I both lost my virginity and became a serious Christian, twin initiations that gave me ample opportunity to consider the relationship between spirit and flesh. Two years later I became a student at Yale Divinity School and several years after that I was ordained a priest in the Episcopal Church.

I wore black clergy shirts and round white collars through most of my middle age without ever giving up the blue jean cutoffs I kept in my closet. Now, closer to the end of my life than to the middle, I try them on again. They are soft as butter. To my surprise they still fit. Looking in the mirror I see how the pounds have reconfigured themselves, chiefly by migrating south. I have not shown this much leg in years. My pale skin has become like thin film on scalded milk. My thighs are lumpy. As old as my cutoffs are, they have changed less than what they now contain.

I could turn away from this image, I know. I could decide to do more crunches, eat less bread, lift more weights. I could cover up in front of the mirror, focusing on eyebrows or teeth instead of less tractable things further down. I could file for separation between my spirit and my flesh. Instead, I decide to love all of what I see. Call it a spiritual practice, since it will definitely take practice. I decide to renew the vows between body and soul.

My parents did their best to protect me from religion, believing that public education, liberal politics, and lots of free time outdoors would serve me better than adherence to any creed. When I was sixteen, I disobeyed them, following my best friend to church one Sunday night to accept Jesus as my Lord and Savior. I was not sure what this entailed, but I had high hopes that turning my life over to Christ would keep my boat safe on stormy seas.

Boys I knew were being drafted to go fight a war halfway around the world. Martin Luther King Jr. and Bobby Kennedy had been killed in such quick succession that I heard gunshots in my dreams. I knew some of my friends were smoking marijuana they were not offering me, while my ripening body became fitted for sex I could not imagine having. I was filled with such grief and passion that when someone told me those were signs of God knocking on my heart, I answered the door. I went to church and got saved.

Since no one told me how to prepare for my baptism by immersion, I followed my own instincts. I read my Bible. I bought a new set of powder blue underwear to wear under my white baptismal gown. I went to church twice on Sundays and again on Wednesday nights while I waited for the date of my baptism to arrive.

When it finally did, I dressed alone in a tiled room that smelled vaguely of ammonia. I walked down more tiled steps to meet the preacher in a pool exposed to the congregation on one side, like a giant aquarium set into a wall. I handed him a piece of paper with my name on it, which he set in the middle of a white handkerchief in his right hand. I said yes to every question he asked me. Then he took a quick look at the name in his hand, held the handkerchief over my nose, and said things I could not hear as he tipped me back into the water.

The preacher was shorter than I was, so the immersion did not go as smoothly as I had hoped. Under the water I could feel his body jerk as he shifted his footing. I reached out for something to grab, but I could not see with the handkerchief over my nose. Between his effort and mine, I made it back to the surface feeling clumsy but relieved. I had done everything I could, and I had done it in front of everyone. I had given my life to Christ.

It was not until I was back in the dressing room that I realized I had also given the congregation a good look at my new underwear. The baptismal gown that had appeared so solid while dry had turned translucent in the water, so that my blue bra and panties shone through like bones on an x-ray. Was I supposed to have worn a dress under that robe? Why hadn't anyone told me?

When I returned to sit with my friends in the sanctuary, I kept my eyes on the pew in front of me, arranging my arms in front of my chest in what I hoped looked like an attitude of prayer. I tried to pray, but every time I got close, my mind ricocheted back to the image of a too-tall girl flailing for a handhold, wet and almost naked at what should have been the most spiritual moment of her life so far. Later, when my teachers in that church told me that the body was fallen and untrustworthy, they did not have much convincing to do. My body had already let me down and I would have a hard time forgiving it.

By the time I got to college, I had left that particular bunch of Christians and was deconstructing much of what they had taught me. I hung out with the theatre crowd. I bought the blue jeans, cut them off, and broke them in. Then I lost my virginity—or, more accurately, I chased a boy down and invited him to relieve me of it—which reopened the confidential file of my body again.

Love was supposed to be free in those days, but mine was definitely hobbled. I did not know what I was doing in bed, and neither did my clumsy partner. Was making noise a good thing or a bad thing? Why was he having all the fun? Clearly, I was a sexual failure. Using drugstore birth control made me feel cheap. I was afraid of becoming pregnant. When two campus evangelists knocked on my dorm room door one night and said the Lord had led them there, I was ripe for the picking. I said the sinner's prayer and renewed my commitment to Christ, becoming a religion major soon after.

I also remained sexually active, combining late-night wrangling with early-morning Bible study. While logic was not my strong suit at the time, the idea seemed to be that the Bible study neutralized the sex. Or maybe I just learned to compartmentalize the two, the way many religious people do? All these years later, the best explanation seems perfectly obvious: I was human. I was body and I was soul, happy to be alive and eager to be fed. My faith and my flesh were not enemies or even opposites; the same wonder that drew me deeper into the first drew me deeper into the second. I could make serious mistakes in this soulful body, but the most serious mistake was to imagine that saying yes to my soul meant living at eternal odds with my body.

The body is not only about sex, of course. It is also about eating, drinking, dancing, running, wearing bathing suits, standing up straight, holding babies, using power tools, driving cars with stick shifts, and playing team sports. I have had trouble with all of these things in my life, not least because I was slow to forgive the imperfections of the flesh. My body was never lovely enough—never flexible enough, graceful enough, fast enough, skillful enough—to win my approval. Even now I labor to find language that does not make my body sound like a useful but stubborn animal that I am trying to domesticate. While I do not hold religion entirely responsible for this state of affairs, most of the language I am letting go is language I learned in church.

Surprisingly or naturally—I can never decide which—I have found the cure for what ails me in the same snake that bit me. If my religion taught me that the body is fallen, then my religion also taught me that the body is sacred. Finding this teaching has taken long years of combing scripture, theology, and church history for the bodily blessings that are there, faint but constant as an underground stream.

In the beginning, the Bible says, "God saw everything that he had made and behold, it was very good" (Genesis 1:31). The Hebrew prophets defended the bodies of the poor as vehemently as they defended the worship of God. According to those who followed Jesus, he was God's word made flesh. Even the Holy Spirit, that airiest manifestation of the divine, loves bodies. "In the last days it will be, God declares, that I will pour out my Spirit upon all flesh, and your sons and your daughters shall prophesy, and your young men shall see visions, and your old men shall dream dreams" (Acts 2:17).

I also have church to thank for teaching me what a sacrament is—a physical thing with a spiritual dimension to it—and for giving me the time and space to get the hang of how sacraments work. In church, they work like this: people bring ordinary bread and wine to an altar where a priest is standing. That priest holds her hands over the small meal, saying thanks for it and telling an old, old story about a night when Jesus and his friends ate such a meal. Next she asks the Holy Spirit to be present in the bread and the wine so people will receive more than calories when they take it inside themselves. Then she offers it to them, holding bread in one hand and a cup of wine in the other.

The people say a simple prayer together or sing a simple song. Then they stand up and walk toward the altar, most of them looking a lot more real than they do at the grocery store or the post office. Some of them kneel down and some of them stand up as they hold out their hands for the bread and the wine. Friends lean against each other so their shoulders touch. Old people's knees pop. Children look up at their suddenly reverent parents the way they look at the moon. Then the people go back to their seats, steeping in the silence while the priest clears the table.

Call me superstitious, but this sacrament worked for me the first time I took part in it. Bread had never tasted so good. Wine had never gone to my heart and not my head. I smelled the wax candles while I knelt there. I felt the warmth of the person kneeling next to me, the embroidered cushion under my knees, the paper-cool hands of the priest who put the bread in mine. I heard the murmur of the words being said over the bread and wine as they were given to me: bread of heaven, cup of salvation, given for you. Time held so still that I could feel my heart bumping inside of me. When I returned to my seat, I felt as full as a glass of living water.

Later, when I was the one saying thanks over the meal and making sure everyone got some of it, the feeling did not go away—I think because the sacrament of communion is a full-bodied ritual. The spirit is not only in the bread and wine, but also in the flesh that takes them in. The sacrament cannot work without bodies. It needs to be touched, spoken over, picked up, handed around, smelled, chewed, swallowed. There is no thinking your way through a sacrament. You have to get your hands on it.

Sacraments schooled me in the wedding of spirit and flesh. I learned how to do the official ones in church—not just communion, but also baptism, reconciliation, the laying on of hands—and then, when I had the hang of seeing the holy in the most ordinary things, I moved on to celebrating the sacraments of picnic lunches, ordinary baths, forgiving embraces, and rubbing sick friends' feet. Once you get the pattern down, there is really no place to stop. Every material thing opens a door to the infinite. Every bodily activity holds sacred possibility. All that is necessary for this transformation to take place is someone to see it and say so, taking one small piece of the world in her hands and saying a blessing over it.

I do not wear black clergy shirts anymore. Like a nun who has given up the habit, I prefer traveling incognito. The downside is that the neck I once hid behind a white plastic collar is now bared for all the world to see. At least ten years older than my face, it hangs below my chin like a crepe scarf that needs ironing—but unlike Nora Ephron, I do not hate my neck. This is my body, complete with pale skin, lumpy thighs, aging flesh. Living in it is the sacrament I know best. Every single day I am presented with the opportunity to wake up, say something kind and thankful over this body, and offer it to the world in a way that promises to be useful. I accept the sacraments of other people's bodies in the same way. They feed me, I feed them: bread of heaven, cup of salvation, given for you.

The blue jean cutoffs go back in the closet, a kind of sacrament of their own. As thin as the denim has become, they knit me to the girl I was, so uncomfortable in her body that I wish I could touch her now, telling her how happy I am to be the inheritor of her capable flesh. Knowing neither the end nor the beginning, my body knows this: this is my soul's home on earth, in which I am pleased to dwell.

The Queen of Hearts

MARGARET GIBSON

Shetland sweaters were a must, but they were expensive, especially at Steve and Anna's, the select little shop in Westhampton where St. Catherine's girls bought their clothes. My mother rummaged in an attic trunk and found a sweater, dusky rose in color, with the large yarn look of a Shetland, and she gave it to me. She had worn it in college, she said proudly, and since I was tall, it just might fit me. Wearing it and my fashionable new shoes—clunky boats of brilliant white leather with saddles of brown and broad white laces—I made my way toward my assigned desk in the Middle School's study hall, avoiding the ring-binder notebooks that edged into the narrow aisle as a few intent girls finished their homework assignments. Study hall was silent at all times, except for morning announcements and morning chapel. I could hear the scrape of pencils, the dull friction of erasers.

The seventh graders sat one behind another in long rows that abutted matching rows of eighth graders. My desk was next to eighth grader Armistead Merriweather, to whom I had never spoken because I only saw her in study hall. Armistead was as exotic to me as a movie star. Her skin looked velvety, tawny. Hers were the largest, most liquid brown eyes I had ever seen. She had fingernails—polished—and a little gold ring. Her clothes came from Steve and Anna's. Our teachers counted on their authority to keep the silence in study hall, but it also helped that to a seventh grader, most eighth graders appeared to be unapproachably mature and experienced. I wouldn't have dared begin a conversation with an eighth grader. When I looked at my seventh grade classmates, I saw the bodies of girls still coltish and unsure. The eighth graders wore their sweaters and skirts with grace and style. Lipstick wasn't allowed at school, but we knew that many older girls had a tube of lipstick hidden away in their pencil cases. Hair combed and lipstick ready for a quick swipe once they were released onto Grove Avenue at three o'clock, the eighth graders gathered at Doc White's pharmacy on the corner of Grove and Maple, to talk with the boys from St. Christopher's. If a boy had a crush on you, he was "snowed." From the bus stop on the opposite corner, I watched the crowd at Doc White's, and like most of my friends, I was gawky, tongue-tied, and envious.

In field hockey, an eighth grader's body followed Miss Fleet's instructions with apparently flawless ease. I stumbled over my stick, failing to send the ball with a confident crack to its destination in the field. How did they do it—Kitty Anderson, Marty Davenport, Lucy Day, Isabel Rawlings? In their short yellow uniforms with bloomers, they couldn't have looked more comical, and yet, given their skill, they managed to give off a gritty allure. Studying them from a distance, I imagined my own body into existence, burgeoning toward a maturity that wouldn't have to think about itself. Eighth grade was the future close at hand, beheld but not grasped.

With a swift, sidelong glance I studied Armistead Merriweather. She was perfect.

Perfect, but not a top student or a top athlete. Perfect, but with a most peculiar manner during morning prayers, the time I had my best look at her. During chapel at our desks, I couldn't take my eyes off Armistead, even though my head was bowed, and my mind supposedly focused on an omniscient and omnipotent God with the same concentration I gave to ungovernable fractions. Together, both grades prayed what we had memorized from *The Book of Common Prayer,* reciting by heart the required General Confession: *Almighty and most Merciful Father, We have erred and strayed from Thy ways like lost sheep. We have followed too much the devices and desires of our own hearts. We have offended against Thy holy laws.*

As she spoke the words softly, Armistead's head bent so low to her desk that her mouth met the wood. Her full, generous mouth opened slightly, seeming to kiss the desk, an open-mouthed kiss that skimmed the surface, not quite kissing, but what else was it? I heard small gasps of breath. *We have left undone those things which we ought to have done. And we have done those things which we ought not to have done; And there is no health in us.* The desk was a dark mirror. I could almost see Armistead's warm breath upon it. Was she kissing herself? An imagined boy? God? Now her mouth opened wider and her lips rested on the wood, murmuring *Spare Thou those, O God, who confess their faults.*

I held my breath as Armistead's mouth married her faults to the study hall desk, her lips wet, her eyes closed, her soft hair fallen over her forehead—she was the carnal embodiment of the words we had recited in the call to prayer: *O Lord, open Thou our lips.* To which we had responded, *And our mouth shall show forth Thy praise.* Whether it was praise or plea, Douglas Noel—and all of us—concluded the confession: *That we may hereafter live a godly, righteous, and sober life, To the glory of Thy holy name, Amen.* As we straightened in our chairs, Armistead looked at me and smiled, gathering her books, making ready to sprint out of study hall to class. Did she know I adored her? Spent from the labor of my attention to her praying, I smiled shyly back and ducked my head inside the slant-top desk to gather my notebook and pencils.

Miss Hood, our history teacher, was a fairy godmother in tweeds, her body a tidy little barrel on bird stilt legs. She wore lace-up shoes that seemed too large for her little body. She wouldn't hurt a fly, if one judged from the sweetness of her face or, less charitably, from the wavering warble of her speaking voice. And yet there was a ferocity to occasional remarks and predictions. "If your parents think the Russians are bad," she warned, tapping a map of the Middle East, "let them look to the desert. *Here* is where the future wars will be fought." She lowered her voice an octave. "Oil," she said, and the heating pipes in the old bungalow, one of the three original buildings, knocked and hissed.

Melissa Banning dutifully wrote down the word "oil" in her notebook. Cookie Lewis was still my best friend, but it seemed as if the classroom seating assignments in Middle School had been designed to part friends and scatter cliques. I saw Cookie only from across the room, rows of classmates between us. By chance or design I was placed next to Melissa Banning in History, Biology, and Math. I was getting used to showing my grades to her at her request when our papers were returned, and she occasionally phoned me at home. Among the first in our class to wear saddle shoes and pleated wool skirts, she seemed to know everyone and even had a friend among the eighth graders, Meade Davidson, for whom the study hall had risked Miss Thruston's ire by breaking into applause when Meade emerged from the bathroom with a triumphant grin which every eighth grader and many in the seventh knew how to interpret. Slight and underdeveloped, Meade was the last in her class to menstruate. Everyone knew she was waiting for Mother Nature to bestow on her the physical maturity which most seventh graders had attained. Her waiting was a physical trial, each month another chapter in a series of suspenseful moments. Her triumphant grin could therefore mean one thing only: finally! Her friends applauded, then everyone else did, Miss Thruston sputtered, shook the wattles of her chin and grew red-faced. "Girls!" she cried. In her maiden outrage and Victorian body, she resembled a hen turkey. "Girls!" Meade, with her childish body and a sophistication of manner than was second nature to her, merely bowed, blew kisses, and smiled.

Melissa Banning, graceful only on the athletic field, was gangly and unformed. In the classroom she twirled a bit of hair with one hand and took notes with the other. She bit the side of her cheek during tests and moved the leg crossed over her knee up and down like a manic wood saw. Often chosen as class captain of the Gold team in our Gold-White rivalries, this year Melissa had been elected president of our class.

"Be careful," prim Kate Pinckney cautioned, as we rode home on the #15 bus. She had noticed Melissa's attentions to me, but would say no more than those two words. "Ask Susan Abbot," she finally offered, closing the conversation firmly. But Susan was not in any of my classes, she lived on Patterson Avenue—too far to visit after school—and she was close to being another one of the outsiders in the class, those mysteriously unpopular, disregarded girls like Patty Wells, Shirley Fairgrieve, invisible Mary Hogue, or Annie Coleman. I tried to figure it out. Was it that Shirley's voice was too shrill, her body too scrawny? Was it that Annie always said the wrong thing and wrung her hands? Was it that Patty's clothes were too small for her and Mary's skin so freckled that she slunk into the shadows for camouflage? Their lack of popularity hung on them like a faint sour odor, untraceable but persistent. They were solitaries, belonging to no group, no clique.

I thought of the scatter of stars in the night sky, some clustered, some far flung and solitary. I thought of jack rocks—the jacks thrown up and spilled randomly on the floor. Some jacks fell into clusters, some skidded off alone, too remote from the others to be gathered in. Considering that I was a relative newcomer to this class at St. Catherine's, I was grateful for my friendship with Cookie Lewis, and I protected it.

Was I going to the slumber party at Bear Island? Melissa wanted to know as we changed classes. *Good,* she replied, when I nodded. Bear Island was the country home of Cookie's grandparents, the Parrishes. Cookie and her cousin Kathy Parrish were hosting a sleepover, and Cookie had invited, predictably, her neighbor Sally Everson and me. Kathy had invited Melissa, Page Fitzgerald, Mary Tyler, and Corbin White—popular girls chosen from the athletic, brainy clusters in the class. It was my first slumber party with a large group of girls, and I was excited and a little nervous, more accustomed to the intimate and nearly familial weekends at the Lewises' house, our rituals of movies during the afternoon and card games at night, and when possible spying on Cookie's older sister Barbara, home from Hollins Abroad. "Baa" was as forbidding and irascible as brother Kent was pliable and sweet.

Kent had to cross through Cookie's bedroom to get to his own. Saturday nights, he would knock, wait, and knock again as Cookie and I leapt into bed, pulling the covers to our collarbones. As Kent, a tenth grader, crossed the room and entered the sanctum of his own room, my cheeks glowed hot, a heat that gradually reached what must have been my heart. Clearly, I was "snowed." Snowed and terrified that Cookie would guess it. Had she known, our friendship might have altered, and I knew that rompish, shy, awkward Cookie needed me as much as I needed her, lest we both be loners to whom no one talked at lunch. The years would pass, I imagined, following the movie in my mind, and Kent would notice me. We'd marry, and Cookie would be my sister until death parted us.

I liked the expression "snowed." It didn't snow in Richmond often, but after gray skies and the rush of snow came winter's clean bright air and a changed world. Snow was beautiful in the air, treacherous underfoot, and like any weather, uncontrollable. You could neither summon it nor dismiss it if it came. When I said "snowed," I could ignore the raw terror and reluctant pride I felt in having a maturing body which, one day, I'd promise to a man. One man only. "Snowed" deferred commitment. In the flurry and rising wind of the storm, "snowed" masked feelings, just as whenever other girls dared speak of sex, they used exaggerated tones of comic and tragic awe to mask what they might really be feeling.

This mixed awe lurked in Melissa Banning's voice as she let me know that Corbin White had promised to bring to Bear Island the book her mother was reading. *Lady Chatterley's Lover,* written by an Englishman. "Just wait until you read the passages that sizzle," she said Corbin had warned, relishing her power to bring us the forbidden. Hadn't I heard that D. H. Lawrence was as randy as he was common? I didn't know what "randy" meant, and I didn't ask. "He writes about *intercourse,*" Melissa said in an impressive whisper.

The deceptive prudery in her voice reminded me of my cousin Nancy Reid, come for a visit in summer from South Carolina, with her salacious tales of blood and barely averted public shame.

"And there I was—Margaret Leigh, there I was, in a convertible—the top down, sun pouring down on us, it was like sliding through town on butter, me in the front seat with this gorgeous *bau-ee,* this divine creature, and right then and there I could feel the blood. It's stained through one Kotex already, it's nearly through the second. He's talking to me about *foot-bawl* and the weekend *paw-tee*—he wants me to wear his class ring on a ribbon around my neck! I can tell he's snowed, he's in a white-out blizzard, and all the while, here's the blood coming! I'm flooding! It's gone through my panties, through the first crinoline—I've got on five crinolines, but it's no good, it's through the next . . . and the next."

She'd been forced to run through her front door, because the blood was just at the last crinoline, brimming toward her skirt. "I just about *died*," she assured me.

I nodded, but I couldn't imagine Armistead Merriweather telling such a story. I couldn't imagine anyone in St. Catherine's Middle School telling it. As if reading my mind, Nancy Reid concluded, "Of course I couldn't tell *muh-ther*. I only told my friends, the closest ones to me at the sleepover. And only with all the lights turned off."

"I wouldn't know," my mother replied when I asked her what was so awful about *Lady Chatterley's Lover*. Why, no one she knew would read such a book! Airy and too easily dismissive, she forgot to ask me why I was asking. Perhaps she trusted me, or perhaps she had something to hide. And so it was with a little guilt that, on a hunch, I searched her dresser drawers the next afternoon as she walked down to Stanley's Market, and I found the forbidden book. It was giving off heat in her slips and stockings. As I turned the pages, reading quickly, I listened for mother's returning footsteps on the front porch. Lady Chatterley's lover was the gamekeeper of her estate, and he lived in a cottage, which she would visit. When they were naked, he touched the two openings between her legs and said, "And I don't mind if ye shits or pisses. I like a woman who can shit and piss." His ruff of pubic hair was red. I read as much as I dared and replaced the book in its hiding place. Then I made a resolve. I would tell her I'd found it, but I wouldn't tell her I'd read any of it. We could both have our lurid little secrets.

"It's not as terrible a book as they say," she told me, after a pause.

"Now don't you tell your friends your mother's reading it!" she exclaimed shortly.

"That man, that man in the book, he really knows what a woman likes," she mused. The smile on her face stunned me. It was tender, as if she had made the man in the book her lover just by reading the book. Mistaking my expression, she added, "Your father's a little rough."

She shouldn't be telling me that, I thought, wishing I hadn't tried to trip her up, catch her in a lie, shock her with my knowing her secret. She possessed, I realized, secrets I couldn't hope to fathom, secrets that tipped into view in the quick lightning flash of words that gave me a glimpse of the woman my mother was, the man my father was. In that flickering light, I'd see but I wouldn't know what I'd seen, and then it would be dark again. Telling me once about her wedding day, she described her dress, the church, Aunt T's house made festive with greens and flowers, the box of baked sweets the cooks sent them off with, the smell of the ocean when she and Dad arrived at Virginia Beach. "We were so happy," she said. Then, "And next morning on the boardwalk I could hardly walk, I was so sore."

She shouldn't be telling me that, I remembered thinking then, too. Mom didn't talk to my sister like this. Mom needed a friend, I realized—and I was it.

Becoming a woman appeared to be a process of repeated shocks and perplexities. I had existed until now in a lull. Until now I had floated in shallow waters. Now the tide was in, bringing with it a stiff undertow, and I was borne by currents I couldn't anticipate or govern. My body had a mind of its own. I could obey Commandments, school regulations, my parents' rules. I could obediently refrain from stealing, I could keep to schedules and codes, I could follow *Proverbs* and not call my sister a fool, I could say "Yes, sir" when my father's eyes darkened and he could no longer be teased by "Poor Daddy, all alone in a house with three women!" But I couldn't ask my breasts to stop growing. I could tweeze the random hairs that sprouted between my eyebrows, but I couldn't ask the month blood not to stain my bedsheets.

In the summer, I longed for the simplicity of earlier trips to Virginia Beach. In earlier years, I would run on the beach, shoot the waves with Dad, eat a full plate of Mom's rare sirloin and new potatoes, roughhouse with Elizabeth and her black cocker spaniel, who chased fiddler crabs into their sand holes on the beach. Now I worried that my Kotex showed in the crotch of my bathing suit. *Take frequent showers,* counseled the pamphlets on female hygiene, but Mom rationed water, Kotex, shampoo. Now at the beach we dressed up in the afternoons and attended "dances" with the famous Lester Lannin band. Invited to dance, or not, all the wallflowers and short boys joined in a daisy ring of follow-the-leader—the band called it the "bunny hop." *Dah de dah de dah dah, dah de dah. Dah de dah de dah dah. DAH DAH DAH.* The rhythm pounded like surf as we kicked and hopped, holding on to each other's waists. I worried that I smelled like rotting fish. Elizabeth and I refused temptations of saltwater taffy and Coca-Colas, spending our money on perfume, powder, bobby pins, and deodorant. Mom and Dad had rented a cottage on the cheap because it was owned by a family whose daughter Mom had taught in second grade. The next week we stayed for free at a cottage owned by Elizabeth's friend Cabell's unmarried aunt. "Divorced, I'll bet," grumbled Mom, looking around the cottage as if for a lurking gamekeeper.

On rainy afternoons, Elizabeth and I stayed in the spare bedroom and listened to the aunt's records, Frank Sinatra singing "Autumn Leaves" and other songs of love and loss. Over and over we played them to drown out our laughter and chagrin as we read Cabell's aunt's love letters, which we'd found bundled and shoved behind the records. They had been written by a Navy man, a sailor. "I'm polishing my white shoes buck naked on my bunk. You should see me!" he had written. Our eyes widened to take him in, and we giggled.

"I think he's a bit too coy," Elizabeth suggested, and we exhausted ourselves in a fit of laughter, avoiding what we wouldn't say.

Committed to being virgins, sworn to virtue until we gave ourselves to the "right" man, we couldn't admit that already we touched ourselves in secret, tasting for ourselves a pleasure we weren't supposed to know lay so near at hand. Until you were with a man, it didn't count, it didn't exist. *Since you went away, the days grow longer . . .* sang Sinatra, and the mournful longing in his voice would all but blot out the image of a suitor buck naked but for his own shoe polish, writing letters to the beloved he wanted with him in his bunk.

Thrown together on vacation, Elizabeth and I were without the refuge of separate friends, separate classrooms, separate bedrooms, and we fashioned an alliance of sorts. "I'm ashamed of my fat," she confessed one afternoon as she tried to conceal her body from my view as we changed into our bathing suits. For once I didn't respond with a fact or observation I'd been harboring to squelch her. I didn't say, "Well, if you hadn't gone and eaten the entire cake on the sly." She had eaten a cake. Just before we left for the beach, cousin Sandra, for whose young children Elizabeth had been baby-sitting, had called to tell Mom just that. I'd waited to hear Mom reprimand my sister, but instead she'd only confided her embarrassment to me. Perhaps Mom wanted peace. She had in April bribed Elizabeth with an early birthday present, saying "I'll give it to you if you'll only stop nagging me." Now I said nothing to Elizabeth about the case of the disappearing cake. Instead, hearing my sister's candid shame, I felt a thrill of sympathy, surprised to feel it, more surprised to be glad to.

"Mom stuffs us," I agreed. Gone was my contempt for my sister's choice of favorite foods—hot dogs, spaghetti, chicken drumsticks, Milky Way candy bars, chocolate-covered cherries, butterscotch almond ice cream, baloney. Gone was my scorn for her plump thighs and calves, her double chin, the soft and pasty white skin of the bulge her belly made, the dimples-in-cream look to the flesh over her rib cage. We had a common goal—to be sleek as movie starlets. And we had a common enemy in our mother, who couldn't help herself—or us—but urged on us fried chicken, mashed potatoes with pan gravy and butter, sausages, batter bread, black-eyed peas, and stewed tomatoes with sugar; our mother, who in Richmond on summer nights several times a week would call out, "Daddy, go and get your three girls double-dip ice cream cones." And she'd call out the flavors she wanted for each of us, the chocolate I found hard to resist, her own peaches and cream, and the butterscotch for Elizabeth.

Quietly Elizabeth and I began to help each other hide food, sneaking half of a sandwich beneath the table to the complicit cocker spaniel, wadding toast into a napkin or a pocket, stuffing fist-sized lumps under cushions or into dresser drawers, reminding each other to retrieve them and throw them out before the mayonnaise turned rancid and the bread blued. It was an uneasy alliance. Elizabeth mocked me with dramatic disgust when I'd wiggle a finger down my throat to make myself throw up. And I'd taunt her when she couldn't resist gobbling half a box of saltwater taffy or chocolates. But momentary slips and stings were ameliorated by our generally united front: we would be beautiful. Thin and svelte, who could resist us?

Returned to Richmond, Mom and Dad increased our weekly allowances so that we might save for clothes we wanted for school. I'd go to Steve and Anna's to look, then take the bus downtown to Miller & Rhoades, buying whatever came closest to what was fashionable in the West End. With me once in Steve and Anna's, Mom placed a mink-cuffed collar, which could also double as a hat, onto my head, stood back, and gazed at me with admiration. It did look nice—but mink? The salesgirl, sensing a sale, closed in with flattery Mom could neither resist nor afford. So that she wouldn't be embarrassed, I adopted a cool and distanced expression, a regal detachment close to boredom. I removed the little crown of mink and flipped it back on its shelf. No, I didn't want it.

And really, where would I wear it? At the dinner table? At the dinner table, nightly the struggles with Mom over calories and serving sizes became a stubborn standoff, which Dad resolved by speaking with his mouth full in a curt voice to demand that we obey our mother. More back talk, we'd be grounded. Sullenly I picked at my food, then gave up and gulped what I was compelled to eat, hid what I could.

I was, in fact, starving, and in school I ate hungrily. Or I took only one forlorn bite of the sandwich and one more of the apple as Melissa regarded me critically. When I said I was too fat, she shook her head and ate a competitively smaller bite of her own sandwich. If I said I was too thin, automatically repeating my mother's pronouncements, she cast a furtive glance of amusement toward any nearby friend. Too thin! Her gaze settled below my collarbone seven inches. Suddenly I understood. No matter how thin I became, no matter how flat my belly, slim my hips, taut my buttocks, I had breasts. I had big breasts, my mother's breasts: I would look just like her. A stout edifice with an expansive front porch.

At home I began to sequester more food, and now not simply to support the alliance I'd made with my sister. I was angry at my breasts and at my mother, the source of my inheritance, never mind that she once mournfully suggested that I should not only be grateful for the engineering of the modern bra, but grateful to have a mother who would buy the bras I needed. As a girl in the country she'd had no money for a bra, and as her breasts lengthened and spread, she had sewn handkerchiefs together to cover them, using ribbons to hoist them higher. Whereas I had earlier responded with sympathy as she described that not quite credible brassiere, now the story only made me angry. She knew what it felt like to be too big. She had felt a similar awkward shame. She, too, had walked into study hall with her head high and her shoulders tilted forward and ever so slightly rounded, hoping to conceal her breasts. Uncertainty she would have disguised as dignity as she entered a room with her notebook held before her like a heavy platter, her cheeks unbearably pink. Mrs. Lewis helped Cookie count calories; Mrs. Banning split a turkey sandwich between Melissa and me and gave Melissa, who was dieting, the "smaller half." Why couldn't Mom help me? Why couldn't she see me?

In order to see myself, I locked myself into my sister's bathroom and took off all my clothes. Hers was the only interior door in the house that locked. I stood on my toes to see more of me in the small, high mirror. I preened. I struck a pose. I touched myself here and there and down there. I closed my eyes and imagined a man who would see me. That's all I could manage to say: a man. I had no boyfriend, no one specifically in mind. Outside the bathroom window, a spring robin bumped and pecked at the window glass, pecked and fluttered, flew away, flew back, fluttered and pecked rapidly, madly, repeating the nonsense over and over, seeing himself as a rival male, or as his own mate, I couldn't tell. I laughed at the robin. Silly bird that couldn't see itself.

Before Cotillions in the winter, I'd sit at the vanity table Mom had bought for Elizabeth's room. She had starched the frilly white skirt, rubbed the glass top to a shine that squeaked. Every Southern young lady should have one, she said. Dressed up and wearing the only shade of lipstick Mom allowed—"powder pink"—I studied my face to see what others saw when they looked at me. The lowered lights in the room made the lipstick appear darker than it was. The vanity table sat where my piano had been moved in my last year of piano lessons. Seated now in my finery, I gazed uncertainly at a face and flesh that were, according to the Preacher in Ecclesiastes, grass: *Vanity, Vanity—All is Vanity,* said the Preacher.

I went to First Presbyterian now, because a few of my classmates went there. Unbelievably, Mom and Dad had allowed Elizabeth and me to change our memberships, and they attended the church with us, keeping their memberships intact, however, at St. Giles. "We're doing it for the girls," I heard Mom tell Floyd Adams when he phoned, puzzled. To change churches for reasons I secretly considered frivolous was vanity, too. I divided my attention between the service and watching other families. I watched Alan Davis and his family in their accustomed pew. Formerly our neighbors on Lexington Road, the Davis family had moved to Three Chopt Road, a better address, and Alan was the smoothest dancer at Cotillion. Louise Hamilton, an Upper School girl whose family was remarkably wealthy, swept into her pew, always late, heavy gold bracelets clanking against the wooden pews when either she or her mother reached for the hymnal. Mrs. Hamilton wore a full-length mink coat. Everything Louise owned was monogrammed—even the door of the turquoise Thunderbird she'd been given for her sixteenth birthday bore her initials. *Better a handful of quietness than two hands full of toil and a striving after wind.* I repeated the words in my mind after the preacher said them. Changing churches made me doubt myself—wasn't this the toil and striving after wind the Preacher berated? And so was this struggle to dress right, dress up, be beautiful.

Before the mirror of the vanity table, I tried to see myself through the eyes of my dance partner, whoever he would be. I tried to see myself as Kent Lewis would see me. As Melissa or Carolyn or Corbin, Armistead Merriweather or Meade Davidson would see me. Only when I saw myself as my mother would see me was I beautiful, and that was embarrassing, because she saw—I had to admit it—herself. "It's all uphill until you're seventeen," she had told me. "And it's downhill after that." Her words were dismaying. I didn't think I was beautiful yet, and I only had a few more years, if she were right, to become beautiful before the gradual decline began. My mother had grayed early, and her breasts had obeyed the laws of gravity, child-bearing, and nursing. She'd told me that "once upon a time" she had been "raahther beautiful," drawing out the "ah" vowel until it was as velvety as her pride.

She had her pride, I had mine, I thought grimly, hitching back a bra strap. At least I hadn't let the girls at the slumber party peer at my breasts. It seemed a long time ago, that slumber party. We'd played strip poker, and I had lost. Cookie, sensing the conspiracy to embarrass us, had thrown in her cards early, complaining that she really didn't understand the game. Too proud for such a claim, which would have been an accurate one, I played hand after hand until I was sitting there in my C-cup bra and panties. This is as far as I'll go, I'd protested. You'll just have to imagine the rest, I'd said, smug the following morning when Melissa was teased about her sparse pubic hair, through which we could see the little mosquito bite swelling itchy and perilously, just *there* on the outer rim of the pubic fold. The nerve of that mosquito.

"It's harmless," Mrs. Parrish had remarked to Mom, who had mortified me by calling to complain about the strip poker.

"They're just at that age, curious. I'd rather have them explore the gifts and perils of the flesh together and at home than . . ."

"Don't they have sisters?" Mom finally laughed.

"Only some of them do," said the woman who had married the man Aunt Billie once had dated. "Don't worry. They're a lot more prudish than we are. We raised them right."

I put down the receiver on the other phone quietly, hoping they hadn't heard me listening on the line as if my life, or reputation, depended on it.

"Women Rule the World," Mrs. McCue had decreed in an Upper School assembly a few years before. The upper grades studied aboveground in Ellett Hall. Now I sat with other ninth and tenth graders in the basement room of Bacot Hall, called Lower Study Hall. If we studied hard, we would rise to the Upper Study Hall, the upper ranks of the school.

Mrs. McCue had retired, but her words had not. Before us was Miss Abbey Castle, her successor, repeating Mrs. McCue's words as, late to the morning assembly by twenty minutes, I whispered my excuses to Miss West before I prepared to slink to my seat in shame. I'd been in the bathroom, sick, I told her. Actually I'd been in the library reading in the stacks and had lost track of time.

Speaking before the lower grades, Miss Castle, Head of Upper School, was busy preparing us for St. Catherine's Day at the end of the month. On that day, a senior voted most like St. Catherine would appear before the entire Upper School in McVey Auditorium, dressed and crowned like the saint the school honored for her faith and for the martyrdom that had elevated her. Miss Castle then repeated Mrs. McCue's famous dictum, affirming the moral preeminence of women in our civilization. Although men might hold the visible positions of power and influence, behind every president, senator, general, and business executive, there was a woman: his mother. Women ruled because, standing behind, like a good wind at your back, women trained the minds and governed the hearts of those children who became the world's leaders. Wives took over where mothers left off. "You are in training to be the 'unacknowledged legislators of the world,'" Mrs. McCue was said to have concluded proudly, quoting an English poet.

I had seen Mrs. McCue's portrait in Ellett Hall, a trim woman in good shoe leather and a wool suit, her face as Scottish as those I would, years later, see in restored photographs of women on the island of Harris, fulling the wool that would be sewn into Harris tweed jackets, like those later worn by the natty fathers of St. Catherine's girls in Richmond. Miss Castle revived Mrs. McCue's words with a gaiety that proclaimed them gospel. Years later I'd recognize that the gaiety, a mask for defiance and resignation, was intended to offer us comfort as we learned to accept our place in the scheme of things. It also allowed the comforter herself to be comforted. At the time, the boast fell on my ears without any slur of complicity. Hearing, I was simply pleased.

Rigorous in their self-discipline, enthusiastic in their scholarship, their aspirations high, their expectations demanding, many of our teachers were elderly ladies who still wore their fathers' names. Miss West, Miss Castle, Miss McKenney, Miss Fitchett, Miss Walton, Miss Keim, Miss Ruffin, Miss Salley. No one called them old maids. Old Maid was a card game; our teachers were authorities to be reckoned with. The celebrated prank of locking Middle School's Miss Thruston in the lavatory adjacent to her class room would not be tried in Upper School. In my new studies, whole worlds were opening to me, and the heralds of the unlocked doors were these maiden ladies who had missed their chances to stand each behind a man and rule. But they didn't need that opportunity to exercise their wisdom and authority. They had us.

In rare moments of daydreaming in class, I studied my teachers.

Miss West taught us Latin. Her hair might be too short, her glasses too cat-eyed, her stomach prominent, her breath bad, but she loved the Latin language and Roman civilization so much, I forgave her transgressions of appearance. Latin she raised from the dead, tracing our English words to their Latin roots, fulfilling her duty to deliver me spellbound to Miss Fitchett's Julius Caesar, Cicero, and Virgil.

Behind those Roman statesmen in togas stood tiny Miss Fitchett, who embodied her name, swatting away the indecisive as if it were a fly.

Behind the Old Testament stood Miss McKenney.

"What did you girls see when your parents read you about Noah and the Ark?" she challenged. I remembered imagining a globe of water, an atlas of flooded plains, a tub-like boat rocking on the waves of the South Pole. When no one said anything, I offered these images, and Miss McKenney smiled. "Good, that's good. Your parents taught you to believe *literally* every word." She paused. "You saw doves and rainbows, too, I suppose." We nodded. I watched the corn-gold stubble over her upper lip, a mustache brilliant in the sidelong sunlight coming in the classroom window. "But that was seeing through a glass darkly."

Again she paused. "Now you must learn the spirit of the old stories. You must learn to see by *metaphor*," and she began to rework the story. I gasped. We had permission to think for ourselves, even about *The Bible*?

Miss Ruthalia Keim, our French teacher, was given to humming Maurice Chevalier as she made a quick turn on tiny ankles, finishing with a wiggle of her ample body. Her bobbed gray hair and bangs fringed an equine face. Down she'd plop, elbows on the low teacher's desk, standing with her generous rear end jutted out, facing the class with her low neckline and elderly cleavage. From this position, smiling knowingly, she'd quiz us on vocabulary, tossing out whole sentences of complex French to us. We had to be daring enough to return aloud a reply in French. *"Je ne sais pas,"* was heresy.

Mrs. Coleman, my only married teacher, taught as sweetly as a grandmother would, gaining her authority through a humility so evident that she became transparent. Reading aloud passages from Dickens or Shakespeare, she vanished, and in her place stood Sidney Carton. Pip. Puck. Lady Macbeth. Through her we met Silas Marner. Jane Eyre. Becky Sharpe.

"You really like reading books, don't you," Melissa said, close on my elbow as we left Mrs. Coleman's classroom. "I mean, you really *do*, don't you?"

She's right, I thought, amazed that her simple, succinct sentence summed me up. I couldn't have said it myself, even though I knew that in the hours I spent reading, I never missed a living human soul. Unwittingly, Melissa Banning had handed me myself. A lover of books. That was who I was. That was me.

"You're what my mother calls a *blue stocking*," she added, but the label—perhaps intended to link me to the fate of an old maid—fluttered away. I knew Melissa well enough by now to recognize her talent for giving a compliment and mocking it with a little sting.

"You're right," I said, disarming the sting with a smile.

Spending more time at her house now than at Cookie Lewis's, I considered Melissa my best friend in the large group of girls that regularly met on Saturdays to play bridge, four tables of us. We had organized the bridge club as our mothers organized theirs—so I was told. In any attempt to emulate our social mothers, I was at a disadvantage. My parents, I realized, had no social life beyond what they'd known at St. Giles, from which they were now distanced. I wondered if they missed their previous participation in choir practice and deacon's meetings, covered dish suppers, and study groups. The thought of their increasing isolation glanced by me and fluttered off. I was focused on my own social life, even though when it came time to organize the bridge club meetings, I stood back and let the other girls make the arrangements. The location of our meetings rotated, and the hostess of the day served a lunch of sandwiches, chips, cupcakes, and Coca-Colas. Corbin White brought her older sister's cigarettes, or if we were in Melissa's paneled basement, finding packs of cigarettes behind the bar was a snap. She had older brothers, and both of her parents smoked.

I learned the game of bridge quickly, taking out books from the library and devouring Charles Goren's column in the newspaper. I loved the sly innuendo of bidding, the discipline of counting cards, the triumph of the trump. A giddy pleasure it was to figure out who held the Jack, who the King, reserving my Queen to cancel the Jack when the unsuspecting opposition played it, protecting her from the King, should that more powerful card be lurking. All of us, the "smart" girls, strove for the ideal bridge table—a game played with savvy and acumen, with no table talk or distractions.

Elizabeth mocked us. It was school on Saturday, she said. Had I made an "A" in bridge yet?

So different from my family, the Bannings fascinated me with their worldliness. Mr. and Mrs. Banning were socially engaged every Saturday night. They went to the Country Club, to the Commonwealth Club, to the houses of their friends for drinks and dinner. They also dressed up, black tie and evening gown. Mrs. Banning descended the basement stairs one evening, ostensibly to remind Melissa and me of a minor duty, actually to display her purple satin dress with a daring single shoulder strap.

I gasped, "You look beautiful!"

Mrs. Banning smiled grandly.

Making a face, Melissa turned away from her mother. The spitting image of her plain father, she did not choose to compliment her mother, who worked hard to remain beautiful. Whenever her mother ate an entire box of Sara Lee cupcakes, Melissa told me, she would perform rigorous exercises—in the nude—in the privacy of her bedroom. Perhaps she wanted to see her indiscretions melting away. We had all seen Mrs. Banning grimly striding up and down Grove Avenue's sidewalks, too absorbed to acknowledge the toots of the horn a friend might sound to encourage her onward. Her curious incivility fascinated me, and I gradually realized that Mrs. Banning wanted to be ignored. She was merely "out for a walk." She wasn't "exercising." A lady was effortlessly fit and trim or effortlessly pleasing and plump. Willing herself thin, Mrs. Banning resembled the grim, angry reaper. She also resembled my mother when she was angry at my refusals to eat, frustrated by her failure to persuade or force down me another mouthful. To be thin, my plump mother asserted, was *unnatural.*

One Saturday evening when Melissa's parents were due to go out for the evening, her brother Henry Banning was hosting a party for his friends, home for the semester. College age, they seemed as remote as Rock Hudson, although not as handsome.

"You girls stay upstairs, let the boys have the basement to themselves," Mrs. Banning advised as she gathered her gloves and checked her lipstick in the hall mirror. Mr. Banning nodded, tossing a scribbled phone number on the hall table. He seemed impatient.

My father had recently gone to Ted Banning's office to sell him tickets for a church raffle. Too hurried to hear out my father's carefully rehearsed words, he'd tossed the required money on the desk. "Sure, sure," he said, looking at his watch. My father, who had grown up with Ted Banning, was incensed. I could imagine him pausing, jaw slack, eyes darkening—insulted. "Don't offer money if you don't really want to go," Dad had told him. I knew the tone of voice he'd have used. Hoarse, shocked, a touch prudish.

"C'mon, Margaret," Mr. Banning said, and my shoulders twitched, as if he might have been reading my mind. But he was only getting after his wife, whose name was also Margaret.

From Melissa's bedroom upstairs, we heard the music of the Kingston Trio, and laughter. A male voice called up the stairs, something about "robbing the cradle." Ill at ease, Melissa kept opening her door and peering over the banister whenever she heard the front door bell. Her brother had promised a modest gathering, subdued and chummy—cards, drinks, a few girls back from college, old pals. Considered something of a disappointment to his ambitious parents, Henry Banning squired about with his wealthy friends, all with reputations for careless banter and the allure of dissolution. Some of these boys had been at Horace Montfort's house the night it burned to the ground in the early hours of the morning. Had a cigarette been dropped in between sofa cushions? No one knew for sure. Horace's young brother had not made it out of the burning house, and so Henry Banning and his cronies had about them the glamour of deadly danger and unpunished guilt.

Melissa and I were playing double solitaire in her room when a knock on the door became a door rapidly opened and closed behind a flustered young woman. "Do you have a phone up here," she cried, "I have to use the telephone immediately!"

She was blond, dressed in good wool, a gold charm bracelet. Her eyes sought ours for comfort or rescue—and remained aloof. We were, she was discovering, so much younger than she. Melissa gave her the phone, and the girl asked if she could be alone in the room when she used it. To my surprise, Melissa said no.

Turning her back to us, the girl began talking rapidly, asking for a ride home. Yes, right away. No, she couldn't call a cab. She wanted to be picked up as soon as possible. She'd say why later. No, she couldn't tell him now.

Handing the phone receiver back to Melissa, the girl asked if she might stay upstairs until her ride arrived. We made attempts at conversation, but she was too nervous to sustain sentences. I remember that she attended Wellesley College. When the front door bell rang, she leapt up and dashed down the stairs, leaving behind the scent of her perfume, the door closing on the abrupt voice of whoever it was who had come to bear her away.

What was it all about?

"I'll bet nothing much," Melissa declared. "She seemed awfully naïve to me."

"She was scared," I suggested.

"You don't have brothers," Melissa said, sounding as worldly as her mother. "I'll bet Goldilocks doesn't either." Then she marched downstairs to talk to her brother. She was chuckling when she returned.

"Not to worry," she told me. "There was a little teasing and Cinderella in distress didn't take it well."

"What did they say?"

"Oh, you know . . . boys. There was a teddy bear downstairs and somebody opened its legs and patted it. No big deal. *May I pat you on the po-po?* Henry asked the girl, and he demonstrated what he wanted to do, with the bear."

"Who was she?"

"A friend of a friend. Girl from out of town, a blind date. I'll bet her friend's dad was put out to have to come pick her up."

I frowned. "What if it had been you, or me? Wouldn't your . . ." and I stopped. No, I wouldn't have found it easy to call Mr. Banning for a ride home, had I been the Cinderella with the po-po a rich boy wanted to pat. But how odd, I thought, how odd that Melissa was responding this way. Of all our friends, she was the one most interested in social infractions. Who was making out on a date? How far did she go? She talked about "getting to first base" or second or third, and "going all the way." You can kiss, but don't tell Melissa was the way one friend put it. We all knew the probable fate of any girl foolish enough to go "all the way." Pregnancy, personal disgrace, family humiliation—it started innocently enough, with a kiss; but that kiss was a flirtation with the devil.

"It was just talk," Melissa insisted. "No one did anything."

"Don't be such a Pollyanna," she said next, more sharply. Then she laughed. "That girl just could have used a little more gumption."

"Women rule the world," I rejoined, glad for a platitude that would cover my confusion.

Had I told my mother about the distressed college girl, she would perhaps have offered familiar advice: the girl needed to have more faith. If you had faith, you could do anything. With faith, any trial might be endured. If you had faith, you had only to wait a moment and God's grace would deliver you. With faith, you could renounce any temptation, sure of success; overcome any loss, certain of restoration. Whenever I listened to my mother echo the words of assurance given from the pulpit, I would shake my head. It sounded too easy. *Only have faith.* Faith and, well . . . a little gumption, and character.

At fifteen, my character had largely been untested. Mrs. Coleman, citing Milton, said that our virtues were "cloistered," and that was just fine, she smiled. We were heroines in training.

Like everyone else, she seemed to think that a girl's virtue and her virginity were one and the same. If that were true, certainly I could agree that I had not yet been tested, and hardly tempted. My "beaux," as my mother liked to refer to them, hadn't been dangerously appealing. Donald Smith had kissed me before a Cotillion, hastily, as if unsure of the sweetness of his breath, or—worse thought—of mine. Lowndes Nelson had phoned to ask me over to Garland Moore's house in the afternoon. They had planned a little music and dancing. Other girls would be there, he said. They were "nice" boys, and so I had bicycled over. Other girls were there; Garland's mother was not. Innocent enough, I thought, and enough *not* that it was interesting. I stayed and tried to do the new dance steps—the chicken, the mashed potato, the tried-and-true jitterbug. Moving toward each other for a slower dance, Lowndes and I were both startled when his hard penis—it had to be that—pushed into my skirt, grazing my pubis. I felt him, he felt me, and we leapt apart as if lightning had struck the floor between us. The shock of contact had been too intimate and, unprepared for it, we looked away, pretending nothing had happened, then danced, careful to keep our bodies far apart.

More recently John Page Williams, the son of a minister with a name my mother ranked "as old as Virginia," was escorting me to the movies every other weekend. We weren't "snowed." John Page was licensed to drive, and when we single dated, he would count "pididdles"—cars on the highway with only one headlight on. When he saw a "pididdle," he said I owed him a kiss. "Who made that rule?" I laughed, but when he parked the car in front of my house—with the front porch light on, bright as stage lighting and meant to discourage the devil's temptations, I let him kiss me.

Leslie would write in my yearbook at the year's close, "Be good with J.P." She might have saved her ink. The temptations offered by Satan, said to be a smooth talker, had left me cold. I was content to wait and see who would enter my life and change it. Wasn't that the plot line?

Waiting, I fixed my eyes on the handsome tenor in the First Presbyterian Church choir, concocting romantic encounters. Not as handsome as Cary Grant or William Holden, nor as polished and misunderstood as Mr. Darcy in *Pride and Prejudice,* nor as doomed as Sydney Carton in *A Tale of Two Cities,* nor as wealthy and decadent as many a European in Henry James, he was—the handsome chorister—at least as distant and more malleable. I thought up what he would say to me and what I would reply. I let his words—my words—swell and roll in my head, where I could be as passionate as I dared, as demure as called for.

It would have been far more daring to summon into my fantasies the boys I danced with, or yearned to dance with, at the boy-girl weekend parties I was occasionally invited to attend. With parents upstairs, teenagers gathered in the recreation room of the basement or in the den, with fast music followed by slow music followed by fast music, the lights lowered or turned back on by the chaperoning parent. These parties netted me at best a waltz with tall Seldon Harris or Benjy Winn, during which I had to be careful not to dance too close because the other wallflowers, from whose tight bouquet I was only temporarily released, were watching to see *if* flesh pressed, *where* it pressed, and *how long*.

Once, just once, Seldon's fingers brushed my shoulder carelessly, grazing near my collarbone, or lower, and I felt between my legs a stupendous flash of yearning. It was sudden, unbidden.

"Sexual intercourse is a communion," as my mother described it. It was sacred. It was like the Lord's Supper. Partaken. Holy. Sanctioned only by married love and sacrifice. I wondered if Mom wanted us plump and unattractive so that the boys would stay away. It would be easier then to keep her daughters virginal. Whether I believed these thoughts or not, fat felt like punishment.

I wondered if the many lovers in the movies were punished because their attitudes toward love-making were not so devout. In wedlock or out of it, women who were too ambitious or too successful—like Eleanor Parker in *Interrupted Melody*—suffered. At the height of her operatic career and married to a good man, Glenn Ford, partaking of life's abundance, she was struck down with polio. Or Jane Wyman, struck blind and having to have her sight restored in a risky operation performed by the man she'd wrongly spurned, Rock Hudson. Or Deborah Kerr, struck by a car as she was running to her tryst with Cary Grant, whom love had reformed from roué to responsible fiancé. They would both have to suffer before they could have each other. In the movies, the suffering gave new meaning to romance. No passion was legitimate without it.

Into a darkened and candlelit McVey Auditorium, the Upper School filed quietly, each class sitting together as a class, waiting for the curtain to be raised on the senior most like St. Catherine. She had been broken on the wheel in Egypt, in Alexandria. The seniors' gold school rings, designed to resemble rings with family crests engraved on them, showed the Crown of victory and the Wheel of pain that were the proof of her faith and love. The voting for the girl who would be St. Catherine had been very close, so said the rumors, and there was a sense of suspense. Who would she be?

The curtain rumpled, rippled, then tugged itself into an ogee arch that made an alcove of light. I recognized the Standard Bearer, kneeling before St. Catherine, dressed in choir robes. She represented our devotion to the martyred saint. I did not, however, recognize St. Catherine, perhaps because of her crown or the makeup, or more likely because she was a boarding student. There was whispering among a few of the seniors. They clearly knew who she was—a girl like them who took Latin or French, who dissected frogs, who played hockey or tennis, and who beyond any worldly accomplishment was well known for acts of tender self-abnegation, doing what was needful, never for her own sake, but for God's.

I liked not knowing who she was. Now I could see the St. Catherine before me, dressed in her long silk dress and crown of fulfillment, as the saint herself, or at least as close as wardrobe and makeup allowed in the transformation of an ordinary mortal who had, in all probability, kissed boys. If you believed the back lighting, the saint was shot through with light from the far side of the world's limits. Before the upright, slender, and awkwardly transfigured image of the martyr, before this living icon that had opened up to an inner dimension with clarity and humility, I felt fallen. I was a sprawl of darkness and division. I was the heart's perplexity incarnate. I pressed further back into my seat in the dark auditorium as the Glee Club and assembled classes began singing "Jerusalem." It was a very strange moment, this one, with St. Catherine radiantly before me—whole, virginal, and inexplicable.

IV

QUESTIONING
Life Without Faith?

Rapture on Hold

RHETA GRIMSLEY JOHNSON

Mother was a woman possessed in the weeks leading up to Christmas. She made candles, using Foremost milk cartons, paraffin from a box, and Number Two yellow pencils with string wound around them to suspend the wicks. She baked. She cleaned. We cleaned at her behest. Every room in the house, including the bathroom, had what she lovingly called "a touch of Christmas."

The boxes came down from the attic, each labeled with what amounted to a cryptic description of Christmas: *Better, store-bought items and music boxes. Nutcrackers and nativity. Candles with glitter. Santa Claus bank and table-toppers. Angel with rhinestones.*

Her enthusiasm was infectious. For weeks I would lie sleepless on the black iron bed—hospital beds they are called—looking up at the blue electric candles in their plastic candelabra that glowed through the curtains in my window. A good little Baptist, I believed the Second Coming was imminent, as sure as spring crabgrass, that is, if Jesus didn't return before spring. And though secretly I never was comfortable with the idea of rising up from this world that I knew and loved, it was clear from the Southern Baptist sermons that we were supposed to rejoice in this idea of going on up to Glory to be with the rest of the saints. So my prayers before Christmas covered all bases and were carefully self-edited, honest in the way you are only if you think someone's looking, careful to make it clear I looked forward to the Rapture, but also getting a plug in for my preferred timetable for Jesus's return.

"Dear God," I'd begin, squeezing my eyes against the aqua electric candlelight burning in the window of our little subdivision house in Montgomery, Alabama. I had been trained to talk to God with my eyes closed, head bowed. It was the only sincere way.

"I look forward to the return of your Only Son Jesus. But could you please wait until after Christmas because I really, really, really want an Enchanted Evening Barbie dress for my Barbie doll? But I will be happy with whatever Santa brings me. Thank you and good night. Amen."

Another year I asked for a delay of the Almighty's endgame until after I got my Visible Horse, the one equine model I didn't have that showed all the bones and guts of a horse through its clear plastic skin, a must-have for the girl who seriously wanted to become a veterinarian. And I didn't know a single girl from eight to ten who didn't want to be a veterinarian. Never mind I had the wrong side of the brain for math and science. I would make up for those mental deficits with a petting hand that wouldn't stop and a big heart. Why, I had a year's worth of *Appaloosa Magazine* under my bed, the pages dog-eared at photos of that spotted champion Joker B. I was halfway there.

I've decided that my Christmas prayer that particular year might have been the only time the Almighty got a message that included a reference to the Visible Horse. At any rate, God obliged. Christmas came and went, came and went, year after year, and the Perfect Man whose birthday it celebrated never once appeared for the party. Thank goodness. For Christmas was far too wonderful to confuse with its Christian origins, too much about the fun of decorating and eating and Santa Claus to entertain a downer like corpses floating up, loosed somehow from concrete vaults, to convene in the sky. That would be better drama, say, at Halloween.

So Mother kept making candles, and for a long while I kept believing in Santa Claus and Jesus, even after third grade when just before Christmas I found my younger sister Sheila's tricycle carelessly and ineffectively hidden in the living room coat closet where, admittedly, few ever dared.

A family meeting was called.

"The parents sometimes have to help Santa with the larger items, things like bicycles and puppy dogs," Mother said with Daddy as her witness. I silently, mentally added "horse" to that list.

I bought it. For another two years—until a friend, who hadn't had proper up-bringing, convinced me that there really wasn't an all-knowing, all-benevolent, all-forgiving man in a white beard riding around in the sky on Christmas Eve. I thus gave up most beliefs in the supernatural at the same time, hiding, for a time, the fact that I'd lost my faith in both Santa *and* God. I didn't figure one could exist if the other was a well-orchestrated fraud.

Turns out, it's perfectly okay, even healthy, to quit believing in Santa Claus. He is, after all, a fictional invention with historical heft only because of reams of literature and art and the abstract hope that there's something more magical to life than meets the eye. It's not so okay, not in these united states, to drop your belief in a god. It gives you instant pariah status, putting you in a despised minority of heretics, misfits, and eccentrics.

When you are young, and Southern, and baptized Southern Baptist, you learn ways to hide your disbelief. I had, in my youth, the all-time best disguise. I hid my budding agnosticism by going to church every time the doors opened. Church was my social life, my chance to dress up, to sing the alto in a tight harmony, to meet boys. There were Halloween hootenannies and Valentine banquets and all manner of choir tours and road trips. The Baptist road trips were where I first learned the facts of life and first saw heavy petting, which the church vehemently preached against. I saw the deacon's son get to Second Base with the preacher's daughter on the road between DeSoto State Park and Franklin, Tennessee, and that moment of choir tour voyeurism remains one of the sexiest moments in my life, though experienced from six seats away. Most of us were enthusiastically singing "I'll Walk With God"—a favorite from our tour repertoire—while the popular couple groped one another in one of the dark back seats. It had all the titillating aspects of forbidden action in a sanctimonious setting.

No bus runs as hot as a church bus.

So what wasn't to like about superficial religion? There was no lie detector test for faith. You went through the motions, kept your mouth shut, and learned to speak euphemistically. And in all honesty, I kept thinking that if I mouthed the words enough, someday I might believe again.

I knew for sure that I was perpetuating a fraud—that I truly did not believe in life after death, much less a literal Heaven and Hell and all the rest—the day our Vacation Bible School teacher, a former missionary to China who had put her tithe where her mouth was, explained believing in the Unseen this way: "When you sit down in a chair, you don't first turn around to see if the chair is there. You simply sit," she said, demonstrating with a choir loft chair.

"Maybe *you* don't look," I thought but did not say aloud. "But if your mother had rearranged furniture as much as mine, you'd damn sure look first."

I probably didn't think "damn" at the time—my cursing facility would come later after decades in newsrooms and hanging around other newspaper reprobates—but you get the point. I still check out a chair before I sit, and that probably has saved me all kinds of embarrassment.

Later, when I left my childhood home and was able to have a social life not sanctioned by Southern Baptists, I still fudged on the belief issue. I might declare I was against "organized religion," which I was, but I never volunteered that it went much deeper. I never stopped conversation in the dormitory rooms, for instance, by interrupting my super-religious suitemate—she spent every free hour of her weekends at the Baptist Youth Union—to debate the very existence of a Supreme Being. I'm not sure anyone would have known what I was talking about. Blind acceptance was so much a part of my culture, American culture, especially Southern culture, that you'd have to have had a masochistic streak to volunteer your maverick belief, or lack of belief.

I was, in a word, a hypocrite, same as those politicians who campaign on some sanctimonious platform of family values while diddling their interns. I suspect the pious Republicans and I aren't the only hypocrites abroad in the land, but I can't know for sure. I can only know my own heart. And I refuse to pretend.

Somehow, despite my inability to embrace the supernatural, I never quite quit loving Christmas, even when I married a wise man who claimed to despise the holiday because of its tendency to aggravate depression and because of its overwrought excesses. Didn't matter. Nobody could talk me into giving up on Christmas.

Every year I still cut a tree and haul around boxes of sentimental decorations and weep over certain ornaments and get chill bumps when Willie Nelson sings "Pretty Paper." I see no reason to deny myself participation in the sport of Christmas, which has become so commercial and secularized that many nonbelievers feel quite comfortable wishing our friends a merry one, making ambrosia, and going completely over the top with decorations.

After all, I am my mother's daughter.

The Only Jews in Town

STELLA SUBERMAN

I was born in Union City, Tennessee, a little dot on the map kind of place in the northwest corner of the state, and we were the only Jews among its 5,000 or so inhabitants, of which more than half were black. My parents had come to Union City to open what was called a "Jew store," and we thought of ourselves as Southern Jews or Jewish Southerners, depending on the circumstances.

In the nineteen twenties and thirties, it was not unusual for lone Jewish families to live in all-Protestant Southern towns. Indeed, it is a story shared by many Eastern European immigrant families who had come to the South from New York and who had in one way or another become the operators of "Jew stores." And it was in these small, often rural, Southern towns that many of us "Jew babies," as we Jew store children called one another, were born and reared.

Though Jew stores had been seen in the South since the late nineteenth century, the Golden Age of Jew stores—the period when they liberally dotted the Southern landscape—was the early twentieth century. And it was during that period, in 1920 to be exact, that my father opened Kaufman's Low-Priced Store in Union City, Tennessee.

I am stricter than some in my definition of a Jew store. I maintain that a Jew store was a modest dry goods store that catered to the lower economic elements of the town—the farmers and the sharecroppers, the factory hands, and the Negroes (as African Americans were called then)—and I further maintain that it had a proscribed stock, which was limited pretty much to family clothing, bed linens, and fabrics (what we used to call "yard goods"). Others argue that any Jewish-owned store located in the South—a haberdashery, a jewelry store, even a general store—qualified as a Jew store. All of us more or less agree, however, that Jew stores were usually one to a town, though it is a point on which I am not so strict: I am willing to say that if the town was growing, another Jew store might decide to try its luck.

There can be no argument about the background of the owners, for they were without exception Jewish immigrants from the *shtetls*—the villages—of Eastern Europe. There is also wide agreement among us Jew babies that the owners—our fathers—had a specialness about them: although they, too, after landing at Ellis Island, had been dumped into the teeming New York City ghettoes, they had rebelled at taking their places as typical ghetto-dwellers and instead set themselves to finding a way to escape. Not all escapees went to the South: some fled to the Midwest, some to the Northeast. A goodly number, however, did go southward, often as peddlers in wagons. And these latter, when they tired of the nomadic life, settled into whatever town they had observed was in need of a Jew store.

My father was not one of the ones who came to the South as a peddler. Although he was indeed an Eastern European immigrant and had lived for a time among the New York immigrant hordes, his method of escape was actually by boat. With persistence he had been hired onto a freighter going he knew not where, but wherever the boat was going, it was all right with him. He just wanted out of New York. It turned out that the boat was heading for the South, and when it got to Savannah and was idling for a moment in the warmth and the sun of that Southern city, my father disembarked and found a job with a Jewish merchant on Whitaker Street.

It was in that store that my father heard of the Jew store tradition, and what he heard made him realize that he might someday operate his own Jew store. He wanted his own store, yes, but first he wanted a wife. Having observed that the Savannah Jewish girls were partial to Jewish boys born in the South and not partial to immigrants born in Russia, he went to the place where Jewish girls did not care if you were an immigrant, who, in fact, knew almost no young men who were not. And that, of course, would be New York. He did not intend to stay in New York—never!—he only intended to find a wife and return to the South. The South had all in all suited him pretty well. Even if he had had a bad moment or two, non-Jewish Savannahians had been mostly friendly, and he was excited by the idea that a good living was to be made in this new kind of land.

In time he did return to the South, but as he now had firm hopes for a store of his own, he did not return to Savannah. Acting on a tip that Tennessee was wide-open for Jew stores, he went instead to Nashville. When he went, my mother and my siblings—by now my brother Will and older sister Minna had been born—went with him.

In Nashville my father took a job as a clerk in one of the city's Jew stores— Nashville was big enough to support more than one—and he soon learned the process for getting a Jew store of his own. Among the things he learned was that the "big" Jewish merchants of Nashville were partners in St. Louis wholesale houses, and as Jew stores were the wholesale houses' bread and butter, the Nashville merchants stayed alert to the possibility of new Jew store venues. My father waited his turn, and before long, the Nashville merchants, acting on a trustable rumor that the Brown Shoe Company was opening a plant in Union City, asked my father if he would like to be staked to a Jew store there, and my father said yes to the men and no doubt gave a "hoo boy" to my mother. The family thus went off to Union City, my other sister Ruth was born soon afterwards, and soon after that, in 1922, it was my turn.

It is a personalized story of Jew stores that provides the main narrative for my book, *The Jew Store,* though in the book Union City is called Concordia, and Union Citians have names other than their real ones as well. To those questioning the name changes in an otherwise factual book, I explain that I did so because of the unsavory folks and incidents I report on. One reviewer who had researched the truth of the book was totally outdone that I had changed names, and the gist of his complaint was that no doubt everybody in the book is dead and there was therefore no need for disguise. It's true that most people in the book *are* dead, but their progeny are not, and I thought to offer a gesture of privacy to all their survivors.

I might also mention that the title of the book was one that did not sit well with any number of people. I know as well as anyone that when the word "Jew" is used as an adjective—"Jew" bread, "Jew" lawyer—there's discomfort all around, but I fought hard for my title because that was what Southerners called these stores, and I thought that this particular bit of history could give no personal offense.

Actually, the term was used by the proprietors themselves. The Museum of the Southern Jewish Experience in Jackson, Mississippi, in an attempt perhaps to shore up my unnerved defenses, very kindly sent me two newspaper clippings from the late 19th century which show ads from two different Alabama stores. One, from the *Clayton Courier* of 1880, says, "The old Jew store is closing, come for the bargains"; and the other, from the *Montevallo News* of 1897, announces, "The new Jew store is opening, come for the souvenirs."

I've also learned that the term was sometimes used in towns not in the South. Indeed there was apparently a store in Kadoka, South Dakota—and I have a picture of that one, too—where on the façade is the store's name, and it is simply a no-nonsense "The Jew Store."

If proof is needed that Southerners often, with no ill intentions, use the word "Jew" as an adjective, I need only to report that when the book first came out, I had a call from the singer and actress Dolly Parton, a good old Southern gal and in fact a sister Tennessean, who was asking for an option to film the book. As she was asking *me* for a favor, she clearly intended no insult when she reported that she had bought a copy of the book, and when she had finished reading it, she said she went out and bought copies for all her "Jew friends."

I wrote the book after a long period of gestation, during which time I held on to the thought that the "Jew store" story was a moment in American Jewish immigration history that nobody was writing about. There were, of course, books and plays about Southern Jews, among them those by the Southern Jewish writers, among them Alfred Uhry, who is the author of *Driving Miss Daisy,* the story of a rich Atlanta Jewish lady and her black chauffeur. Miss Daisy did indeed live in the South, but no credence should be given to any similarity between the life of Miss Daisy of Atlanta, Georgia, and the Kaufmans of Union City, Tennessee.

There are many differences. First and foremost, Atlanta was—and is—a city so rich with Jews that it provided, and still provides, an array of temples and synagogues catering to most every kind of Jewish economic class and philosophy, and with this abundance of things Jewish, Atlanta was definitely not a typical Jew store town. Jew store towns had no synagogue, no temple, or, as my mother would say, "no really nothing Jewish." Furthermore, I daresay that both whites and blacks of Union City would have thought that Miss Daisy and her black liveried chauffeur had descended from another planet. Jew store towns had no well-spoken black chauffeurs who drove rich Jewish ladies around. If in Jew store towns there were well-spoken blacks, I never knew one—the education system for blacks being what it was, which is to say completely dysfunctional— nor were there any rich Jewish ladies. Jew store towns were, in fact, places where most of the residents had never before seen a Jew, rich or poor.

The writer Eli Evans has written of his town, Durham, North Carolina, but Durham was likewise atypical, most strikingly because one of its Jew store own- ers, Mutt Evans, was the town's mayor. Mutt was, in fact, mayor not only once, but six times. Mutt always explained his success by saying that Southerners re- spected anybody who was strong in his religion—whatever religion—and Mutt definitely was strong in his. When I think back to the Jew store owners I knew, I recognize that they were town presences, but mayors? I don't think so. I can only explain Durham by noting that Durham was big enough to have a synagogue or two where a Jewish merchant might demonstrate his religious resolve.

Much as I admired Alfred's and Eli's work, I understood that Eli and Alfred were writing of events and people unknown in Jew store towns. Jew store towns had their own unique dynamic, and it was played out by two very disparate groups—rural or semirural Southern Protestants on the one hand and immi- grant Jews on the other. And powering the dynamic was the struggle to find a way to connect when the usual means of connection—similar beliefs, customs, language—were largely unavailable.

In Union City, among the 2,500 or so white Protestants, religion was in a very dominating position. The church was a considerable part of the lives of my friends and their families, and their conversations were filled with talk of "the church." They all had a church, and unless my friends had chicken pox or the measles or their parents were down with something—"lumbago" was a popular ailment—they went to church every Sunday without fail. On Satur- day mornings, my friends went to play games in the backyard of the church, and on Saturday nights they went to church for potluck suppers. Their mothers had their "church group," which had charitable works in mind, and they met in their churches one afternoon a week. Their fathers met weekly in their various churches for Bible class.

Religious words and phrases were always in the air. My friends, most notably their parents, had biblical sayings and homilies at the ready, and they blessed me often. In most any conversation the Lord Jesus was sooner or later called upon, frequently sooner *and* later. When I had dinner at my friends' homes, not an uncommon event, I knew not to eat until grace had been said—offered "in Christ's name, amen"—and grace was the prelude to any partaking of food, even Union City's favorite lunch—a banana and mayonnaise sandwich on white bread.

In my friends' homes, religious tracts filled the magazine racks. My friends all knew their Bible, and some knew it by heart. My parents became aware of this in their very first encounter with a Union Citian, a nine-year-old boy who had helped them find a place to stay, and when my father had asked the boy, quite rhetorically, if it wasn't written somewhere that a little child shall lead them, the boy had replied without skipping a beat, "Yes, sir. Isaiah 11:6."

Church buildings commanded the landscape of Union City and represented almost every Protestant denomination. The Episcopal Church was the one exception, a circumstance due to the standing of the Episcopal Church in the Southern church hierarchy. In the South, the Episcopal Church is the upscale one, and Union City was not the kind of town that could support an upscale church.

As to synagogues, when my family arrived in Union City, they already knew they would find no synagogue. Indeed, it is part of family lore that when they were taking their first look at the town, as they passed by the churches, my mother began counting, and when she got to seven, she said to my father, "All these big ships, and the Kaufmans don't even got a rowboat."

If this heated Protestant community accepted us, it was because my parents, like all Jew store proprietors, were determined to get along. There was no mystery to it: getting along was key to making a living. To this end, Jew stores cooperated in every way possible: when civic support was needed—for a church drive, to send a young person to a county or state competition, to provide an award for the school's best speller—the town Jew store always came through.

In personal ways, my father and mother approached "getting along" differently. Because of his stay in Savannah, my father had had a leg up on understanding how to manage with non-Jewish Southerners. He had learned, first of all, that he must be known as an honest tradesman, but he had also learned some other things, and one of them was that personality counted. And personality in this particular circumstance meant an ability to banter and "to take a joke." They were qualities that came naturally to my father as they no doubt came naturally to all successful Jew store owners.

My mother learned more slowly, but in the end she learned. She, too, had natural qualities and talents, and they turned out to be useful. She was a person who appreciated kindnesses—perhaps because they had been so rare in the rough-and-tumble of New York—and though kind gestures from her non-Jewish neighbors did not come at once, they did come. They came first as offerings of plant cuttings, and then there were other offerings, and my mother replied to them, if in her own way. Having learned to sew at the age of eleven when she had left school for employment in a New York garment factory, she ran up items on her sewing machine—mostly handkerchiefs and aprons, but sometimes really tricky-to-make sunbonnets—and sent them over. She was little by little learning to get along.

She learned the social customs and soon knew that she must take her turn. She *reciprocated,* as my oldest sister Minna, who had quickly tuned into the ways of the South, would call it. Since we were invited to every Easter egg hunt, we gave one in our own yard. At a neighbor's house, my heart leaped up when Santa Claus handed presents to Ruth and me, and I delighted in running around the neighborhood handing out our own Christmas presents. And yes, we had a Christmas tree, though it was just a limb taken from our backyard pine. The Christmas tree gave my mother pause, and when she wondered if it was sacrilegious, my father would say, "Don't worry, Rebecca. That tree is so puny God won't even notice."

If neighbors invited us for some sort of home entertainment and refreshment—maybe listening to a program that their radio could "bring in" but ours couldn't—my mother issued an invitation to something at our house, perhaps a piano recital by my older sister. At a neighbor's house we would be "refreshed" with iced tea and a pie whose crust was not as flaky as it might be because, in deference to my mother's sensibilities, the neighbor had made do with Crisco and not lard; and at our house, the refreshments were as requested by the neighbors—hot tea and rugelach, my mother's buttery little fruit pastries.

As my mother and the neighbors minded each other's babies and sat on each others' porches waiting for the doctor to come in times of sickness, my mother was discovering that non-Jews could make good neighbors and that she herself could be one. And if my mother was aware that through the years a few of the neighbors continued to look at her with some want of confidence, she was also aware that some looked at her with simple curiosity, as if they were eager to know what "being Jewish" was all about. And many looked at her with true understanding and affection. As my mother herself said later, "We all opened up our eyes and let the light come in." I don't know exactly how that works, but we knew what my mother meant.

As part of the learning process, my mother was also finding that despite herself she could tolerate many things, to the end that my siblings and I were on a very loose leash. When a baptism was scheduled, though she herself stayed home, she allowed us to go with the crowd to Reelfoot Lake to watch a Baptist get dunked, and if there was to be a christening, we could go to church to watch a Methodist get sprinkled. She had no objection to my going with my friends to their Sunday schools, where I colored pictures of Jesus and Mary and, occasionally, of Joseph, or to the evangelists' tents to watch town and county people fall on their knees and declare for Jesus.

For me, Sundays were not, as Eli Evans has called his own Sundays, the "loneliest day of the week." For me, Sunday was very special. Sunday was a day that started with my getting dressed up to go to Sunday school, and afterwards to Sunday dinner at a friend's house, the prelude to which was a dash to the Holy Roller church to peek into the windows to glimpse all the writhings and wrigglings. And not to be overlooked was the dinner itself: fried chicken made extra-delicious because it had been fried in the vaunted—and taboo in my house—bacon grease, and collard greens that had been simmering away all morning on the stove with a chunk of fatback—"seasoning meat"—nestled inside. And, always, beside my plate a glass of iced "sweet" tea and for dessert a slice of lemon meringue pie. I knew to expect that after dinner the family would settle into a reading of the Bible, and it was then that I would go home to my own family and play card games for hard candies. Who could ask anything more of a Sunday?

Since my mother's philosophy seemed at this point to be that though we might be different, she would see to it that we were not *too* different, she enrolled me at the Presbyterian Church's preschool, the Sunshine Girls, which most all Union City (white) children attended.

Still, it must be said that her leniency went just so far. I could eat pork in other people's houses, but I was not to expect it at home. I could not have a cross around my neck. I could not have an Easter dress of organdy with a big bow at the back and a matching bow on my head. I could not have a picture of Jesus over my bed, and my mother did not encourage me to say prayers at bedtime as my friends were wont to do. I could not sing hymns for my aunts when they were visiting from New York.

And so, little by little, though the differences remained, the differences became less and less important, maybe even more and more interesting, and as we lived those years in Union City, my father's store prospered, my mother had neighbors she trusted, and we felt we were not only tolerated but liked. Still, about Jews in general the townspeople had mixed feelings. And this was because what these little towns knew of Jews came from a combination of the Ku Klux Klan and the Bible.

The Klan, as the self-appointed protectors of white Protestants, was very active in our part of the state. When we went to town gatherings, the Klan often presided, and we listened while they gave us the word. Chiefly, they told us whom we should guard against. First on the list, to nobody's surprise, were the so-called "colored races," and the Klan warned us sternly of the danger of allowing them to "mix their seed" with ours. Next came the RomanCatholics, which was pronounced as if it was one word because "Roman" suggested "Rome" and Rome was that fearsome city where the Pope "was sittin' up there bein' more important to RomanCatholics than even our own President." Not that anybody knew any RomanCatholics—had ever *seen* any RomanCatholics—but the Klan advised us to stay alert in case of a sneak attack.

The Klan had Jews on their roster, where they were listed as part of the phrase, "Jews and other foreign-born." Were they talking about us? If they were, why was this so? We knew them all: some lived on our street and one delivered our milk. And didn't all of them like to banter with my affable and helpful father? Yes, they did, and indeed my father would say that if the Klan marched on us, they would march in sheets bought at our store. So after a while we tried to convince ourselves that the Klan wasn't talking about us and wouldn't bother us, but it seemed to me that my father was never sure.

The Bible as a source for information on how one should feel about Jews was most unsatisfactory. On the one hand, the Bible was telling New Testament Bible-readers that their Lord had been born Jewish and that the Jews were God's chosen people, and this was a real plus for Jews. On the other hand, their Bible was also telling them that the Jews had killed their Lord and were to be cursed forever, and this was a definite minus. What to think?

I was also confused. My father had always explained to us that it was the Romans who had nailed Jesus to the cross, "for political reasons," as he said. So what was I supposed to think when I heard so often that Jews had killed "our Lord"? There is no doubt that a part of me thought that I must be responsible somehow. The sight of a cross showing poor Jesus hanging from it always gave me a guilty twinge, and of course in Union City I saw many a cross with Jesus, nails in his hands, writhing in agony. I think now that if I felt this guilt—and I certainly remember that I did—a question must follow: Did those who took to heart the words of the New Testament think that it was only just and proper that I have such feelings?

In terms of my own religion, whatever my participation in Christian practices, however familiar I was with the rites and ceremonies, the thought was always with me that this was my friends' religion, not mine. I was not a Baptist, footwashing or regular; I was not a Methodist; I was not a Holy-Roller. I was not any of the other denominations I was so familiar with. The activities that I joined in with my friends at their churches were to me just another way to have fun. I may not have set foot in a Jewish house of worship until I was a young teenager, but it never occurred to me that I was not Jewish.

I have no doubt that I knew I was Jewish from the moment I was born, for my mother would have suggested it with a word of two even as I lay in my cradle. She might have called me her "sweet little *Yiddishe tochter*," her sweet little Jewish daughter; or she might have said that I was her "*Yiddishe* bit of *tsuker*," her Jewish bit of sugar, which when you think about it, was a combination of Jewish and Southern sweet talk.

And it was true that my mother tried to maintain a connection with Jewishness, or *Yiddischekeit,* as it is called. She even tried to "keep kosher," though she knew it was a hopeless goal. She couldn't depend on a rabbi, since the closest one was in Nashville, which was 150 miles away, so she would put the Friday night chicken through her own kind of "koshering." She didn't try to "kosher" other meats, but chicken seemed to her in desperate need of koshering, and she set my father to killing one of ours so that it could end its life in glory as a koshered bird. My father, of course, did not kill the chicken as the rabbis did, with a knife specially designed for the purpose and with designated places on the chicken's neck for the plunging and the cutting. No, he just wrung the chicken's neck. Afterwards my mother placed the chicken on the drainboard and let its blood drip into the sink, and my father would say that all the taste of the chicken was draining out as well, and my mother would answer that it was more important to have "kosher" than taste. Not that she was satisfied with her koshering. She could not hope that her prayers over the chicken would carry as much weight with God as a rabbi's, but a rabbi was in Nashville, and she was in Union City. *Oy!*

On Friday nights—the beginning of the Sabbath—my mother made an effort to present a traditional Friday night meal, and she lit candles and with a shawl over her head mumbled a blessing over the *challah*—the Jewish egg bread— in the rough Hebrew she had learned by rote. She had made the *challah* that morning, and it had sat all day on the side table in the dining room, its braids glistening in the light. The pièce de résistance was, of course, the chicken, which had more than done its share: it had first been boiled to make soup and then had been put into the oven to brown, after which my mother gave herself permission to call it "roast" chicken.

Yes, I knew I was Jewish, but that was about all I knew. My parents were basically unable or unprepared to speed me along the way to a real understanding of what it meant to be Jewish. Since my mother's knowledge of Judaism consisted chiefly of the trappings—a broad understanding of it considered to be in the province of males—she could not provide much religious sustenance. Even the words she spoke in her Friday night prayers were not just a mystery to my siblings and me but to her as well.

As for my father, he was not only not religious, he was irreligious, a nonbeliever. And he gave no quarter. He didn't forbid my mother her indulgences, but he most definitely didn't support them and indeed often spoke loudly against them. In response to her continued longing for the Jewish community that a synagogue offered, my father's answer was always that Jew store families were in towns like ours not for religious "entertainments" but to make a living.

My mother never challenged my father when he said such things. Did she feel she had enough faith for two? Or was she simply following the European/Jewish tradition of obedience to the man of the house? My feeling was that she did it out of her unbounded respect for my father.

Much of this respect derived from her feeling that he was much more *American* than she was. She was proud that he had lived in Savannah and had learned there how to live as a Jewish person in the South. She thought he spoke English without an accent—"like a Yankee you speak," she had said to him when they first met—and it was almost true. That his English was good was due in large part to a Savannah women's group that had put "Teach Morris Kaufman English" on their list of projects and, faithful student that he was, he had improved his English substantially. But did he speak without an accent? Well, how often when he was speaking of George Washington's home did I hear "Moun Twernon"?

Whatever her reasons, she just gave a little indulgent smile and turned away when my father laughed at religious "rigamarole" or railed on about belief. Actually, although my mother came from an Orthodox family where her father wore a yarmulke all day every day, where rites and ceremonies were strictly observed, and where the synagogue was central to their lives, she and her siblings, like others of the newer generation, had let things slide a bit. This generation was following the new norm, and the new norm held that if you were going to succeed in America, you had to modify your behavior to suit American realities.

My father, however, went well beyond behavior modification. His small five-foot-six-inch frame held big opinions, and he shared them with us often. And we children listened. When my father said, as he did often, that God was "just a rumor agreed on by everybody," my mother might smile and turn away but we children wanted to hear the rest of the story. We wanted to hear about his fellow *shtetl*-dwellers in Russia and how they said that in America the streets were paved with gold, that in America on the day you arrived you got a job and a new suit of clothes and a big bed to sleep in. And my father, with no little derision, would then ask us, "Did they see? Did they know?" To which his answer was always the same: "No, of course not. It was all *schmontses*." All nonsense.

My father was always suspicious of the golden streets and the smart clothes and the soft bed. He was doubtful from the very first time he had heard tell of them. He felt it was all wishful thinking, and this was confirmed when he came to America and found only a job delivering coal that paid 25 cents a day, which allowed him to rent a space on the floor in the corner of a room in a relative's apartment. "When those *kalichers* talked about America, where were their facts?" he would ask. "Those know-nothings had no facts, only dreams." It was those doubts that my father carried with him to his attitude toward the existence of God.

I do not know for sure what went on in the homes of other Jew store families, but I suspect many of those fathers had opinions similar to my own father's. And I also suspect that if they did, they behaved as we did and kept those opinions behind the family door. Surely we were all aware that these attitudes would not be welcomed in our towns. Though a slight bit of agnosticism might be tolerated, might even become the subject of good-natured joshing, a statement of nonbelief was not acceptable, not ever. And the truth was that if we were to get along in the community, it was imperative that we share the values of the community, and belief in God was a very important—perhaps the most important—value. We were well aware that for those who expressed views opposed to the town's prevailing one, a very specific punishment awaited, and it was a "running-out-of-town."

I was terribly intimidated by these "run-outs" and saw many a picture of them. Folks in nearby towns, along with snapshots of lynchings, sent us snapshots of "run-outs," the subjects of which were white families in wagons, their belongings heaped about them, being chased to the county line. "Run-outs" had motivations different from lynchings, which were meant exclusively for blacks, but they were almost as popular.

Since Union Citians were confident that they met the "belief" criteria, "run-outs" were not much feared by them. But the Kaufmans couldn't afford to take a chance. It was one of the things we knew without discussing it. And so my father's opinions on religion were kept close. Did we know if anyone else in town shared these opinions? It should go without saying that there was no way to know.

Even if we had longed to practice our religion, doing so was virtually impossible. Since our closest synagogue was in Nashville, in those days of impassable roads, one hundred and fifty miles was unthinkable. More to the point, however, even if the trip had been possible, for business reasons we would not have gone. Our store, like all stores in the South, was open on the Jewish sabbath—Saturday—and closed on Sunday, unlike the Jewish stores of the North, which held to an opposite schedule. Saturday was our big day, and we typically stayed open until past two in the morning. And since my father was indispensable, there was no thought of going somewhere to attend services, not even for the high holidays. Even my mother accepted that attending services was out of the question.

But sooner or later push had to come to shove. And so, if my mother had accepted compromises, if she had managed in Union City to make peace in most respects with her religion, there were still a couple of issues that did not lend themselves to compromise and they were waiting to be grappled with. One had to do with my brother Will, and one had to do with Minna, Ruth, and me. And both issues were, to my mother, nonnegotiable.

The issue with my brother was a big one. It was the Bar Mitzvah, and it was unthinkable to my mother that Will not participate in the traditional Jewish rite of passage to manhood. "A thirteen-year-old boy and no Bar Mitzvah?" she would cry. "It's a *shonda!*" To which my father would say that it was not a decision to be ashamed of, it was a sign of clear headedness.

But my mother stayed strong, and she had a proposal: Will would be sent to her parents in New York, where he would study and then have the Bar Mitzvah ceremony. My father, of course, had his own proposal, and it was that my mother forget about it. "Send Will away?" he would thunder. "For what and for why? To be away from the family for years and for something nobody knows what?" Still, he finally got the message—that my mother was not going to back down and that he was going to lose—and the result was that Will went off to New York, where he stayed for a long time. When he came back, it was for "visits," and though we were awed by his tales of New York, we had to adjust to having a brother again, which we never quite did.

It was interesting, however, that during Will's visits home he became the toast of the town and was much in demand as a dinner guest. It was his knowledge of Hebrew that did it. Union Citians were thrilled with his fluency in "the language of our Lord," as they said, and who better to give the blessing at supper than a speaker of Hebrew? Will always obliged, and as he set about to give the blessing, the father of the house would say to his flock, "Children, I want you to listen carefully. Will is speaking the language of our Lord." Afterwards my brother, who had learned a few things, would explain to us—to us alone— that the "language of our Lord" was not Hebrew but Aramaic, and my mother would say, "Never mind. It don't hurt anybody to think that," and my father would say, "It always hurts not to know the truth."

When my brother had left for New York, though it signaled the end of one issue, another was waiting. The other issue involved husbands, and husbands involved us girls. In my mother's mind, Jewish girls married Jewish boys and that was all there was to it. But where, oh where, would those Jewish husbands come from? We were three Kaufman girls, and finding three Jewish husbands in our little corner of Tennessee would have required the beating of many a bush. My mother's answer to this dilemma was—what else?—we would go to New York.

The issue entered crisis stage when my oldest sister Minna came into marriageable age and—*oy vey!*—became romantic about a local boy. And now my mother, her anxieties at fever pitch, confronted my father a second time, and now my father simply took a deep breath and capitulated, so aware was he that his argument—that his girls could be just as happy with gentile husbands as with Jewish ones—would send my mother into what we called in Union City a hissy. And so he took himself out of the fray and allowed my mother's needs to take over, which meant that our days in the South had come to an end. It was good-bye to the Jew-less fields of northwest Tennessee and hello to the Jewish hotbed of New York.

Did my sisters find Jewish boyfriends. Yes. Did I? Well, I was a young teenager and didn't much count. But did being in New York influence my religious views? Did attending, finally, a synagogue inspire in me a longing for a faith, a religious belief? I have to say it didn't.

In the synagogue, I sat with the women in what I called "the balcony," while the real business took place below among the men. What the "real business" was I hadn't a clue because I had no idea what the Rabbi was saying. And neither did the women around me. The Rabbi read in Hebrew, which the women did not know, and when the Rabbi spoke in Yiddish, though the women now understood, I was still pretty much in the dark. I did get the general drift of his message, however, and though it included thoughts on the role and needs of Jews in the community and in the world, its main theme was what God had to say—in other words, God's strictures and demands.

In the balcony, as I sat thinking about all the talk about God, suddenly to my ears came my father's questions—"Did they see? Did they know?" They were the questions he had asked when he described for us the *shtetl*-dwellers and their belief in the golden streets of America. As I remembered those questions, as they rang in my ears more and more loudly, I asked the same questions of those in the synagogue, those who spoke and those who listened: Did they "see," did they "know"? Apparently I was, like my father, a stickler for evidence.

I guess I'm still a stickler for evidence, though I often hear from others that evidence is overrated and that faith can exist without it. They chide me that I haven't left myself open to the "faith" experience, haven't allowed myself to accept that there is something beyond evidence. It's a "feeling," they say, even occasionally a "voice." They claim to have experienced it in one form or another, and they express pity for me that I haven't. "Sometime when you least expect it," they say, "God will speak to you. Have faith."

The vocabulary is different for nonbelievers. Nonbelievers do not talk about faith but about hope or confidence, the level of which depends on the level of the evidence; and they talk about marvels, not miracles. "Faith" and "miracles" infer a supreme being, and a self-actualizing supreme being is not part of the thinking of nonbelievers.

I have found among Jews many who feel as I do, many who share my lack of belief in a deity. When I was on an author's speaking tour, I visited a Jewish temple in Detroit whose Rabbi had been on the cover of *Time* Magazine, where he was called "Detroit's Atheist Rabbi." I'm not sure the members call themselves "atheists"; I think they call themselves "humanists." Still, they are all Jewish and all nonbelievers, and they seem to enjoy both of these designations. Perhaps they feel as I do—that being Jewish, being part of an ethnic group, adds a dimension to one's life. I agree that the dimension is sometimes a challenging one, but sometimes it brings one into a marvelous tradition.

In situations where believers use the word "religion," nonbelievers often use the word "tradition," and I am one of the ones who do this. It helps me explain why, even as I reject the most important tenet of Judaism, I still call myself Jewish; and it helps me explain why I feel a strong kinship with Judaism. Is this the "spiritual" experience that others hope for me? Perhaps it is, if "spiritual kinship" infers a tradition and not a religion.

I have wondered about this interest in tradition. Just as I am not a religionist, neither am I a sentimentalist who revels in tradition for tradition's sake. It took some time for me to understand, and I found understanding in the words of one of my heroes, Albert Einstein, who is perhaps a hero also of the folks in that temple in Detroit. I found his words in his answer to the question of why he, on record as a nonbeliever, still considered himself Jewish. What he said was that "the pursuit of knowledge for its own sake, an almost fanatical love of justice, and the desire for personal independence—these are the features of the Jewish *tradition* which makes me thank my stars that I belong to it." [Italics mine.] Did I *qvell*—shiver with pride—when I found those words? Well, yes, I did.

I hear often about the downsides of not believing. Prominent among them is the idea that nonbelief leads to immorality, and I wonder if believers in their heart of hearts really subscribe to this. Is it conceivable to them that most people are upright only because of fear of retribution from the Almighty? It is a concept unacceptable to me. Did those folks in that little town in Tennessee who loved Jesus but loved us as well treat us with respect and kindness only because God was judging? What I believe is that when Union Citians solved the original dynamic—the struggle to connect townspeople who had never before seen a Jew with a Jewish family who had never before lived among Southerners—it was by the simple application of the Golden Rule. What I believe also is that most of us—believers and nonbelievers alike—if left to our own instincts and able to free ourselves from corrupting forces, live our lives by that message, the one that says, "Do unto others as you would have them do unto you." It is a way of comporting oneself that I believe is intuitive to all humans.

It seems to me that the Golden Rule serves very well. Although the concept originated in Greek philosophy long before the Bible was written, many Christians first find it in the Bible. I, too, "know my Bible," as my Union City friends would say, and I read in Matthew 7:12, for example, the words of Jesus Christ as he spoke of the way to honorable behavior, and I embrace his words with all my heart. His words were, simply put, his version of the Golden Rule.

The Golden Rule's message is one of which my father would very much approve. "See how easy it is?" he would say. "You want to be a *mensch,* you don't listen to no monkey business. You do what you know you ought to do." And I would agree with him that if you want to be an honorable person, you have but to listen to your own better voices. But I expect that my father would say more. I expect that he would also say, "But let me tell you, you don't need all that rigamarole to be a *mensch*. Rigamarole never made a real *mensch*. A real *mensch* doesn't need *entertainments*." And would I also agree with that? Well, yes, I think I would.

A Purposeful Life

MITZI ADAMS

As a young girl, I enjoyed picking blackberries, fishing for bream, watching the real stars . . . and the man-made ones. I'd spend hours relaxing on the warm asphalt of the road that went by the Sweats' cabin at Lake Lanier. I was quite safe there (except perhaps for the odd venomous snake), since there was little traffic on that road in the sixties and probably even now. But during those times, because the population of Atlanta was only about 200,000 and relatively far away, when the Sun went down, it was very, very dark and if we so chose, the only lights were from the fireflies (we called them lightnin' bugs). So, the stars were bright and many, the Milky Way was bright and easy to see, the planets were easy to spot, and the Moon . . . the Moon was incredible.

Sometimes against the black background of space, I'd see those odd tracks across the sky that disappeared into the shadow of the Earth. Satellites, they were called, satellites that had the potential to watch what we were doing, to drop bombs on us, or to monitor the weather, to determine the productivity of farmland, to discover remnants of ancient civilizations, or other parameters of our environment. I even saw *Explorer I,* the United States' first satellite, data from which confirmed the existence of the Van Allen radiation belts. At this time in my life, I hardly imagined that I would later meet and become friends with one of the men who pushed the button that put that satellite into orbit. Watching these points of light traverse the sky, I saw the potential to explore, the potential for the human species (and especially this one individual) to move off planet Earth. Although my generation was faced with the possibility of destruction by atomic bomb and thoughts of global destruction were frequent, I imagined that through space exploration, we might just possibly preserve our species (and the other species that inhabit Earth), and that we would someday expand into the solar system and the universe.

Watching *Star Trek* IN COLOR was a real treat and a good reason for me to stay in the good graces of the Sweat family. After watching *Star Trek* at the Sweats' house on Lake Lanier, I'd sometimes take out their small-refracting telescope to look at the Moon and the planets. The next day I'd create my own space-exploration stories. As I walked about the shoreline of Lake Lanier, I fantasized that I was abducted by the crew of the *Enterprise.* Of course, I would be the intern of Mr. Spock; my best friend, Cindy Winstead, would be the intern of Captain Kirk. I fantasized that the crew of the *Enterprise* thought I was worthy enough to be part of the crew . . . and they took me (us) away with them. At this point in my life, I was about thirteen and a major event occurred: my parents divorced.

I suspect that the divorce of my parents was a great influence on the development of my philosophy of life, as was reading books by Ayn Rand, Kahlil Gibran, and others. The independence of the women in Ayn Rand's books appealed to me. Gibran's philosophy espoused in *The Prophet* gave me comfort and an understanding, perhaps, of one reason my parents could not get along. About marriage, he said, "Love one another, but make not a bond of love; / Let it rather be a moving sea between the shores of your souls." My mother's "bond of love" probably drove my father away from her.

As most thirteen-year-olds do, I thought a lot about life, the universe, and everything. While a baby with no choice, I was christened as a Presbyterian and, through my youth, attended McElroy Memorial Presbyterian Church on Clairmont Road in Chamblee, Georgia. Around the age of twelve, though, I began visiting other churches. My parents laid down only two constraints: no visiting Catholic churches, no visiting Jewish "churches." My neighbor down the street was Baptist, so I visited his church. I didn't like it. As a ballet and tap dancer, I really didn't fit in there, since many Baptists frown on dancing. Another friend was Methodist, so I visited her church. I liked that one and joined the Methodist church at around age thirteen, gave my life to Jesus, and set about being a good Christian.

First of all, I didn't feel different. God wasn't talking to me, and as far as I could tell, if he/she had spoken to me, I would have been carried off to the crazy house. Further, God wasn't answering my prayers, especially regarding my parents' separation. And anyway, how does God decide to answer *my* prayers, but not my next-door neighbor's? So, I rather quickly began experiencing conflicts with my "new life." I saw so many inconsistencies in this and in most religions. On the one hand, "thou shall not kill"; on the other, God is commanding one tribe to kill another, including even the animals, the women, and the children (*e.g.,* Deuteronomy 20:16–17). I shared my concerns with one of my life-long friends, Billy Mitchell, who was also a member of this Methodist church and also a "questioner."

Billy and I had a long history of "discussing things." When the movie *2001: A Space Odyssey* came to Atlanta, we viewed it at the theater and subsequently had endless phone discussions, attempting to understand the underlying message (we'd also read the book) of the movie. Billy fed and fed on my interest in logic and the scientific method. (As a naive youth, I believed that because of logic, scientists would always make carefully thought out decisions based solely on logic . . . boy, was that wrong; scientists are human, too.) In addition to the movie *2001,* Billy and I talked about the Big Bang, evolution, the existence of God, social injustice, the existence of an afterlife, and we frequently brought these discussions to Methodist Youth Fellowship (MYF) meetings on Sunday evenings. We brought up points such as, "Why is it that a Buddhist, who won't kill even a roach, will not go to heaven, but that a 'Christian' who is an adulterer, who cheats on his taxes, who speeds, and thinks he's entitled to go as fast as he can on the highway, will?" It seemed to us that the Christian was a Christian (or Muslim was a Muslim) simply because of where he or she was born. If some-one was born in the Christian part of the world, he or she had the opportunity to "be saved" and to participate in the "true" religion—a kind of religion by geographic default. It seemed to us that because of this concept of a "true" reli-gion, these organized religions ultimately contribute to world conflict.

As you can imagine, my ideas and Billy's were not shared by our fellows. We were not particularly ostracized, but our views did set us apart. The discussions in MYF meetings could be summarized by the following: In science and logic, there is an agreement of rules of analysis of the world and an emphasis on analy-sis. In religion and spirituality, the rules change with the individual and with the ruling party, and there is an emphasis on emotion. Heaven help you if you were Jewish in sixteenth-century France. And if you were not Catholic during the reign of Queen Mary, you might have been burned at the stake. If you were not Protestant in the Southern United States in the 1800s (or even in the 1960s), you might not be burned at the stake, but you wouldn't exactly be instantly trusted.

My childhood was not idyllic, but comfortable, and my upbringing was fairly typical of the suburbs of Atlanta. Although the socioeconomic status of my family in the late 1950s and early 1960s would have been considered to be lower-middle-class (*i.e.,* we were poor!), we had a black maid when I was young. The maid cooked and cleaned and performed the duties of a nanny. I often wondered why she was treated differently than white women and why she couldn't live close to us. "Doesn't Jesus love her, too?" I'd ask my mother. When getting on the bus with my grandmother, I recall asking, "Nanny, why does that black man go to the back of the bus?" Heck, I even remember wondering why that *white man* gave *us* his seat. I guess I was recognizing inconsistencies in my Christian upbringing, which may have also contributed to becoming a feminist at a very early age.

During the upheaval caused by my parents' divorce, there was upheaval in the world: the Vietnam War, Kent State ("Four dead in Ohio"), and always the possibility of *the Bomb. I* wanted Logic to rule. In spite of this, I had a curiosity about the possibilities of extrasensory perception. Was this curiosity a thinly veiled desire for power, or was I trying to connect with God? Either way, this question still remains: What is mind? How does the brain create the mind and the person? We seem to use so little of the physical brain (or so research in the 1970s suggested), might there be extra abilities lurking in those areas of the brain/mind that we rarely access? After all, we know from quantum physics that somehow distant particles seem to be able to communicate with each other. Isn't that telepathy of a sort? In my brain, at the quantum level, could particles send or receive information over long distances, instantaneously?

Over a thirty-year period from 1935 on, Dr. J. B. Rhine conducted experiments on ESP at Duke University. The data from these experiments suggests that ESP is real, but the Rhine experiments, to date, have not been precisely reproduced, a requirement of the scientific paradigm. In spite of this, I would *like* to be able to directly communicate with others (language is so imprecise). I would *like* to be able to transport myself instantaneously from one location to another (cave diving in winter would be so much more pleasant). I would *like* to feel truly connected with another. Isn't this interesting? Logic is important to me, but I want to *feel* connected with another. So perhaps, in *my* universe, logic must work with emotion. But in truth, all humans must evolve to work more effectively with both logic and emotion; otherwise we won't survive.

I am a cat lover. Actually, I'm an animal lover, but particularly I like cats. Currently, I have five feline companions, two of whom are eighteen years old. So what about my feline companions? Do they have "mind"? Do they have "soul"? The Bible tells us to be "good stewards" of Earth but Genesis 1 tells us to "be fruitful and multiply; fill the earth and subdue it; have dominion over . . . every living thing that moves on the earth." Living with my five furry-feline friends in North Alabama, I know that I don't have dominion over them. I experience every day their individual personalities and long memories. In this, they are similar to me. But because some phrases in the Bible suggest that humans should have dominion over all things that move on earth, somehow animals other than human become lesser beings. The human, now disconnected from the rest of nature, can mistreat the dog or cat or pig or dolphin or whale or wolf. The world becomes man's plaything and whole species and their habitat can be lost as man *conquers* nature. But in doing this, humankind is shooting itself in the foot. By destroying species, habitat, and diversity of species, we may be destroying ourselves.

To provide for my cats, I must feed them a diet with a lot of protein (although less as they get older). Proteins are broken down by the stomach to provide amino acids; cats must have a specific one, taurine, to survive. Cats in the wild learned to survive by killing, sometimes not efficiently, sometimes cruelly, but hunting and surviving are a necessity for them since they evolved to need taurine, which cannot be provided by plant proteins. In this way, I am different from my cats; I can choose to eat only vegetables. I can choose to grow my own food, to grow it sustainably, or to eat only locally grown produce. Raising cattle can be much more expensive than raising vegetables, and knowing this, I can survive pretty happily on peas and corn and peppers and potatoes. So I wonder why modern humans still choose to eat much more meat than they need, which uses many more resources than needed. If we view this Earth as an isolated globe in space as all we have, we are much more likely to protect our resources. But if we use Earth's resources from the perspective of being outside the ecosystem with a view only for personal gains with the assurance that all is "God's Will," we risk destroying our planet.

As a young adult, I believed that technology and science and logic would solve the world's problems. But it seems that knowledge, learning, scientific thinking are no longer respected. If decisions are based on faith instead of logic, how do we determine whose faith is the correct one? In a country like the United States with Catholics and Muslims and Protestants and Jews and Buddhists, it is imperative that decisions impacting the entire country not be made on "feelings" or "beliefs." For example, I am often asked by friends and family if I "believe" in global warming. The answer is that I have seen *physical evidence* (rising global temperatures) that supports the idea that the climate is changing. This is not a "belief" any more than the idea that Earth revolves about the Sun is a "belief." Measurements have been made that support the hypothesis. To date, there are no conflicting data, at least about the rising temperature. Decisions about the future of our planet must be made based on the data, not on feelings or faith. For even if humans are not the cause of the rising temperature (this is where the conflict is), it makes sense to reduce emissions simply so that we have cleaner air to breathe.

In addition to the loss of physical resources, I am concerned about the loss of mental resources. We recently lost two major scientific minds and good men: Ernst Stuhlinger (2008) and Konrad Dannenberg (2009). These two men were a part of the von Braun rocket team that developed the rocket that took twenty-one men to the Moon. Although some have criticized these men because they contributed to the German war effort during World War II, to my mind, they were visionaries. Von Braun was even incarcerated for a short time by the German military because he was more focused on going to the Moon than on the war effort. Ernst Stuhlinger was a gentleman scientist who loved astronomy and exploring. I knew Ernst personally, the man physically responsible for pushing the button that put *Explorer I* into orbit, and although I knew him less well, Konrad Dannenberg was an excellent engineer; in his second (or maybe third) career, he was a great teacher and ambassador for space. But it's important to realize that even with the accomplishments in the 1960s that resulted in humans planting their footprints off planet Earth, we cannot, at this time, reproduce that work. The reasons for this are many, but funding plays an important role. In 1968 (the first Apollo landing on the Moon was in 1969), NASA received 2.4% of each tax dollar. Today in 2009, NASA receives 0.55% of the total federal budget or about one-half penny of every dollar. That half-penny supports planetary, astrophysics, and heliophysics basic research as well as aerospace research *and* the engineering efforts to create a launch vehicle that would take us back to the Moon. There's just not enough money to go around. But it's not just about money. After the early 1970s, we lost much of the expertise; we are now permanently losing the experience. The life of an individual human is so short. We work hard at school, succeed at a career, retire, die. What happens to the memories and experiences of that individual? Again, what is mind? Wouldn't it be so much more efficient to transfer memories and experience from one human to another, so as not to lose the expertise of a lifetime? Could this be the next step in human evolution, possibly assisted by human technology?

Life, individual life, is it important? One would think that perhaps the Ernst Stuhlingers and the Mother Teresas are, but what of us normal individuals? I rescue a cat; that's important to the individual cat, but the feline species will not progress or change because I have intervened, *especially* since I intervened, because all my cats are altered. However, *my* individual life is enhanced and improved because of my interactions with that one cat. These interactions spur my appeals to the rest of society to create conditions that will sustain as many species as possible and, in addition, to create the conditions in which humans will learn to live peacefully and sustainably alongside the other species of Earth. So perhaps my individual life *is* important. This life, this is the life I must live as fully, as rationally, and as ethically as possible.

From prehistoric to historic times, a role of religion in society has been to supply rules for living, creating order from chaos. One way of assuring that religious laws would be followed was to threaten consequences in an afterlife. But the Romans gave us secular law, which kept order in the world by punishing transgressions here on Earth. Derived from both religious and secular influences, modern ethical ideas developed. I personally do not need the concept of a God or even the rule of law to know that stealing from another is wrong. I can empathize with the individual who is victimized and know that I wouldn't want to feel that way. Further, threats of punishment in an afterlife make no difference to me since, following my rational mode of living, I have no evidence for the existence of an afterlife. From the evidence, it seems that we have only one chance to live a purposeful life, which can be done without being a part of organized religion and without a god; we should make the best of it.

V

TRANSFORMING

Faith in Change

A Fairy Tale

The Prodigal Daughter Returns

CONNIE MAY FOWLER

She had been drawn to the little sea shack nestled betwixt water and sky with the simple purity of a turtle whose true north is a singular spot of sand on an empty beach. She was happy there. The details of her life—errands into town, cleaning the house, writing her books—were timed in conjunction with the comings and goings of the Gulf because she loved to wander the beach at low tide and marvel over treasures the sea had momentarily left behind. On this sandbar she called home, she felt in touch with the Goddess-spirit, with the eternal circle she viewed as sacred (life feeds death; death feeds life). Troubles seemed less ponderous and joy less threatening in the presence of nature's rhythms.

But even the beauty and steady honesty of this place could not save her in the aftermath of that soul-wrecking divorce. The absolute anguish she felt over the slow death of her marriage and the venomous tentacles that grew from its corpse forced her into a dark and hopeless internal landscape. Physical proximity to the sea could not assuage the wasteland her heart and its attendant need for well-being suddenly occupied. Old friends could not help. Family could not help. Possible lovers could not help. No one could help. The past and its malignant vestiges poisoned the present, infected the future. With her spirit in exile, she acted on what she viewed as her only reasonable option: she fled. She ran inland, not unlike Nick in *Remembering Blue,* and immersed herself in the task of becoming whole again, cell-by-cell, moment-by-moment, blind-eye-by-blind eye.

She decided to teach. It was a good thing, this teaching life. She met eager and brilliant young people, their hearts still untainted. They reminded her, in all their innocent vigor, that hope was still present in the lives of many people. She met women who understood the ways of a brokenhearted sister and they quietly walked with her down paths she was fearful to travel alone.

But there were villains afoot all along this path, and her sisters could not always protect her. Predators smell wounded prey and, as is sometimes the way with life, she arrived in this place far from the sea deeply, deeply wounded. Nonetheless, for a few years, she managed to outwit the villains, but the odds in this urban land of red tooth and claw were stacked against her. She did not heal fast enough. Her wounds and her naiveté were too entrenched, too obvious.

In the early hours of a late summer day as she slept, someone she knew broke into her home and attacked her, body and soul. The police, the counselors, the victim advocate, the state attorney sang in unison, as if a Greek chorus, "Yes, it's almost always someone you know."

All the work she had done over all the years to recover from her past (battered children grow into adults who are wracked with self-revulsion and doubt) was undone when her attacker, by word and deed, stripped her of her dignity by violating her bone-by-bone.

Her undoing had just begun. Someone who considered himself a leader among men, a real shaker and maker, a mouthpiece who had loudly proclaimed throughout this landlocked place that he was her staunchest ally, turned out to own a jagged heart made of thistle and stone. In the wake of the attack, when she was at her lowest ebb, he—just for the sport of it—shouted to all who would listen that she had asked for it, that she was lying, that she was unstable, ungrateful, unfit because women who claim they have been assaulted are nothing more than little Eves: beautiful, dangerous, apple-loving liars.

Once more, she found herself relegated to a lightless place, standing dumbly, taking sucker punch after sucker punch, no one hearing her howls for help; she had forgotten that sometimes the only person who can help you is yourself. But she did acquire a stubborn question: How does a person live peaceably with himself when his greatest pleasure is to pummel a woman after she is down?

Our prodigal daughter, it turns out, was stronger than anyone, including she, realized. Fed up with taking the blows, fed up with asking for justice in a place populated with enablers (if this were a traditional fairy tale, written by a wizened old witch in a forest, she would have used the word "twits" instead of the psychobabble inspired E word) who were too fearful to listen or act (hear no evil, see no evil, get no bad press, who among the players on this stage is most likely to sue?), she rose from the blood and gravel her attacker and enemy had tossed her in, and she did so simply by acknowledging her innate goodness. Sometimes the simplest decisions require the greatest courage: She would not, she decided, allow herself to be defined by the violence, cowardice, and cruelty of a few petty tyrants posing as demigods.

At first, she wasn't sure if she would survive. Strangers walked up to her on the street and asked if she were okay. Trusted former students who lived hundreds of miles away, not knowing what she was going through but prompted by hidden angels, phoned and told her it was time to move on, to take care of herself.

"Time to ascend, baby!" one of them said.

This tale has many holes in it . . . it's not a story, really, more of a thumbnail sketch posted in the wind. The books, the oral history, the pen-to-paper art will come later. But rest assured the tale has a happy ending . . .

Our heroine left the land that two villains had smeared with the blood of her good nature and returned home to the shanty, and the sea, and that big, big sky.

And what about now? How is she in this new moment?

Listen.

Once more her heart and intellect are tied to the comings and goings of the Gulf. Dolphins glide by as she conjures her next story and the birds, she is sure, are happy to again be getting three square meals a day.

New doors are opening and she increasingly feels strong enough to walk through them. That is how she met the man who would become the great love of her life: she opened a door and, taking small but hopeful steps, reentered the world.

With her heart filled with an abundance she had feared she would never again experience, she wanders through North Florida's piney woods to be met by old friends with open arms who are surprised, yet not, to see her *(we always knew you'd be back)*; who sweep her up, who tell her they love her, who whisper how happy they are that she is finally home. Home. It is a beautiful word, she thinks. It sounds like the yogi's *ohm*—vibrant with the possibilities only peace brings.

She sits on a spit of sand that is, by turns, a turtle crawl and the Gulf's fine belly, and realizes she is breathing differently. Each inhalation and exhalation bears an ease born of regained happiness and an urgency prompted by a renewed will to live fully. It is an odd juxtaposition of grace and want. She has, by tragedy's swift, surprising hand been made aware of mortality's awesome shadow—how quickly it can overtake and obliterate. But the awareness does not suffer her. Everything she learned out there in that vicious yet unbearably tender world serves her well. The lessons—enduring, hard won, and treasured—amplify the core tenets of her nature. In greater measure than before she left this place, she is quiet, strong, determined, loud, contemplative, patient, impatient, wise, stupid, funny, curious, and wonder-filled. She is insistent about both *carpe diem* and *laissez les bons temps rouler*. She is kinder, slower to judge, but also less tolerant of resident evil.

As she sifts the sand between her fingers, she breathes in the yogi's tiger breath—is nurtured by it—and hums a homily to sky, sea, dolphins, and her present self, "Home. I am finally, finally home."

THE END

Alice Walker Calls God "Mama"

An Interview with Alice Walker

VALERIE REISS

Alice Walker has always known God. But she prefers terms like "Godness" and "Mama" to describe the divine—for her, it is everywhere, from the Japanese maples outside her window to the slow yoga she practices. Though her seven novels, including 1982's Pulitzer Prize–winning *The Color Purple,* and many essays and poems have myriad themes—from feminism to race to class to love—a palpable sense of Mama's richness runs throughout, as well as fiery resistance to any force that attempts to control or contain this juicy, abundant, and ever-present divine.

In her most recent book, a collection of political, spiritual, and personal talks, essays, and meditations, *We Are the Ones We Have Been Waiting For: Inner Light in a Time of Darkness,* she calls *The Color Purple,* a "Buddha book that's not Buddhism." Recently, the author talked to Beliefnet about meditation, activism, and how we can all bless ourselves anytime, anywhere.

In which sense did you intend the word "meditations" below your new book's subtitle?

It's political meditations. Politically, the world is so confused right now—there's so much suffering caused by various movements by various parties and people in power in government. And many people are truly overwhelmed even thinking about politics and the environment and world affairs, so I wanted to offer thoughts on these, but I also wanted to give meditations after each section, because some of the information is a little difficult. A meditation eases that a bit.

How can people stay compassionate while still being knowledgeable and active?

There's a saying that I appreciate a lot, which is "Knowing without doing is not to know." That seems to be where most of us live. We say, "Oh, I know that." But if we don't do anything about it, do we know it? I don't think so. And so, part of practice for all of us now should be understanding what exactly we know, and the way we tell what exactly we know is to notice what we do.

How do you know that you're knowing?

The last essay [in the book] is about being arrested in front of the White House in 2003 with these other wonderful women against the war. It was one of the happiest days of my life because I knew that I knew, and I knew that I knew that I hated war.

What kind of meditation do you practice?

All kinds. At one point I learned transcendental meditation. This was thirty-something years ago. It took me back to the way that I naturally was as a child growing up way in the country, rarely seeing people. I was in that state of oneness with creation and it was as if I didn't exist except as a part of everything. And that is where meditation can help you understand yourself.

What's your meditation ritual?

Over the years it shifts. I used to meditate all the time in bed. That was when I was raising my daughter and I'd get her up and off to school, and then I would go back to bed, and meditate. And then I would do the same in the evening, and that was very good for that period because I had so many things to juggle as a single mother. But now, I can meditate walking by the ocean. I can actually meditate driving. Not when I'm in traffic, you'll be happy to know.

At least not with your eyes closed.

No. I'm just saying that there are certain activities that lend themselves to the meditative state, and it was quite astonishing that driving happened to be one of them. I sometimes take long drives from here to Mendocino, which is north of Berkeley, and when there is no traffic, it's just amazingly meditative. And so, the whole point is basically to be in yourself, to not resist whatever needs to be worked on in yourself, to let that rise, to let it come and to look at it as closely as you can, and then let it go. And I sometimes say that meditation is like flossing your mind . . . you get rid of a lot of stuff that you actually don't need to continue carrying around with you.

Do you also practice yoga?

I do. I met this man who recently sent me a whole instruction book and tape and everything about Yin Yoga. This one is just right for this time in my life. You concentrate on the inner parts of your body, like your bones, your tendons, not so much your muscles. And it is wonderful. You stay in each pose for five minutes. It seems like a long time, but it is so good because we get really cramped in our daily world.

You wrote in this book that The Color Purple *was your Buddha book without being Buddhism. Can you explain that?*

Well, Buddha was Prince Siddhartha and he lived in a castle. And one day he discovered suffering and old age and death. And then he decided to try to find a better way to deal with this.

The Color Purple is about theology. Many people assume that it's just about incest, wife abuse, spouse beating; all of that is in there, but you will notice that the journey that Celie is making is toward her self-realization as a part of the entire Godness. Speaking of God as everything there is, was, ever will be.

When you close your eyes and tune into God, what do you see?

I don't close my eyes. Why would I close my eyes? It's everywhere. I mean, it just is. What is this if it's not God?

Do you feel like your whole life you've had a sense of God in this way?

Yes. I do. In fact, when I was thirteen, I stopped going to church because I felt like they had taken this huge, amazing, incredible Godness and whittled it down to this tiny little thing that they stuck in the church every Sunday when people were too tired really to listen, and fell asleep because they were exhausted from still being slaves, basically.

And I wanted, and I insisted, even at that age, on going out into nature and truly feeling what is there, what—you know, we're not—you know, the reason we are not alone is that—because earth is with us. We are her beings. It's not because there's somebody in the sky who's watching us, you know?

Do you have a preferred word for God?

I like "Mama."

In the book you talk about a chant and mudra [yogic hand gesture] that Spirit gave you. Can you explain what that is?

It's a way to bless yourself and to give yourself some sign that you are protected and loved. And as we go into this part of our journey as a planet that is quite frightful, actually, I realize that we also need something that is a gesture to bless ourselves.

So, the mudra is to hold your thumb and your two first fingers together, and then to circle your heart, or you can circle your whole body while you say or chant, "One earth, one people, one love." And this is very good to say for seven times while making the mudra around your heart and your body just as a way of calming yourself, centering yourself in the reality of being this one place, earth, and this one people, the people of earth.

Do you have prayers that you say on a regular basis?

"Thank you" is the best prayer that anyone could say. I say that one a lot. "Thank you" expresses extreme gratitude, humility, understanding. People pray and pray—and that's fine. But, for me, "Thank you" just basically says it all.

Who are some of your spiritual gurus?

Well, I have teachers. I like Pema Chodron, Jack Kornfield, Thich Nath Hanh. I like a lot of the spiritual teachers out of India. I learned from Jesus when I was a child. I was very taken with the stories of His life and very much taken with His struggle to bring a new way to His people. I'm very delighted to have the Gnostic gospels and the Nag Hammadi scrolls. And I'm just constantly delighted with the Dalai Lama and the ancient, incredibly wonderful teachings that have made their way to America from Tibet.

You talk about silence a lot—how has that also been a spiritual and creative teacher for you?

Everything does come out of silence. And once you get that, it's wonderful to be able to go there and live in silence until you're ready to leave it. I've written and published seven novels and many, many, many stories and essays. And each and every one came out of basically nothing—that's how we think of silence, is not having anything. But I have experienced silence as being incredibly rich.

Do you ever have dry spells or writer's block?

I don't believe in them. I think that if there are periods when you're not do-ing something that you're used to doing, it means that you can spend that time doing something else. If I get up and I think I'm going to write something and it's not there, rather than sitting there and trying to wait for it or try to give it a little nudge, I think, "Oh, I can do something else with this time." And then, there's so much else to do.

Do you have other creative outlets?

Oh, yeah. I paint. I garden. I dance. I cook. I farm. I have never felt that the one thing that I am "known for" is what I am.

How are you feeling about aging at this point in your life?

Well, I'm sixty-two and I feel wonderful. I have loved every decade. I had a little rough bump in my thirties. And the twenties were politically very rough. I think it's a very good thing to be entering elderhood and to take that role in my family and society. I love life even more as I see and have seen so much of it.

Oprah played Sofia in the Color Purple *movie and helped produce the Broadway show. Why do you think she's so popular right now?*

Oh, I think that she is like a contemporary goddess, actually. Which is different from saint because saints have to be good and perfect, and she's not interested in that. She's interested in doing good things, but how she behaves and who she is is her business, and that's very goddess-like. I think that she offers people a lot of help and a lot of aid and a lot of inspiration and a lot of joy.

In the book you quote Martin Luther King saying that the saddest words are "It's too late." Do you think it is?

Well, it depends on what you're thinking it's too late for. It's never too late to start trying to bring peace to yourself and take that into the world, which is what I try in my life to do, because I really do understand that, unless you have it in yourself, there's no possibility of giving it. That's why you can't make war on people and think that you're bringing peace. It's just ridiculous.

And what's your greatest hope for humanity?

Well, I hope we can wake up. If we can rise to the challenge that our global interconnectedness gives us. I sometimes talk about how the people who wrote the Bible didn't know China existed. But now we really can connect with all the places. We can see cause and effect. We know about karma. We know karma is just that, that, if you do something mean to somebody, it's very likely they're either going to do it back to you or they're going to pass it on to someone else.

We have a splendid opportunity, for the first time ever on earth, to truly get to the root of things and to transform human society. It's entirely possible, and it's really up to us. And since I believe that, I don't worry about it because I know that we will either do it or we won't. If we do it, "Hallelujah." The world will just be so wonderful and joyful. If we don't, we will lose such a beautiful gift. And I will have to say that while I was here, I did my very best and loved it as much as it loved me—the cosmos, the earth. I personally feel like I'll be fairly content. You can only do what you can do. It's just a fact that worrying is unhelpful, whereas trying to bring peace to your own spirit is work you can do, and it's work that will actually bring many benefits to everybody that you ever encounter and to the whole world.

Signs of Faith

BARBARA ROBINETTE MOSS

About twelve days after I got home from the hospital, my preacher friend Garret drove down for a visit. Though he lived in Canada, he had grown up in Alabama. We understood each other in ways that only Southerners can. It's knowing that fried okra is fabulous no matter what other people say.

I was on the couch with a blanket, even though it was hotter than Hades, and Garret sat in a wooden rocker, his hands in his lap. I had downed pain meds so I'd have the strength to talk. I was furious and I wanted Garret to fix it.

"You think you've been good so you can't understand why God has let this happen to you," he said.

I tugged at my blanket defiantly. "That's exactly what I think. What's the matter with Him?"

"You can't be *good enough* to get into heaven, Barbara. You know that's not how it works."

"I'm not talking about heaven," I snapped. "I'm talking about *right now*. God could have stopped the tumor a long time ago, or healed it."

Garret sighed. "God doesn't work that way."

"Why not? If God is God, why *can't* He work that way?"

"Don't you see? Everybody could say that. Why doesn't God *fix* this?"

"Well, why doesn't He?"

Due to my weakened condition, Garret decided not to argue with me. He lifted a gift bag from the floor and brought out a folder. "I don't have the answers, Barbara. I'm a preacher because I've got some of the same questions myself." He opened the folder. "I brought you some things that might be helpful. Here's Internet information on all the churches in your area. What kind of service they have, what denomination." He handed me the folder and I flipped through it, wondering if he knew I no longer went to church. Except for Easter Sundays and Christmas, I hadn't been in years. It seemed to me that churches didn't do what they were supposed to do.

Once, years earlier, the church I belonged to faced a crisis. The city planned to build HUD housing two blocks away. The deacons held a meeting and decided that if they couldn't get the city to change their plans, the church would build a privacy fence around the church property. That Sunday the congregation was told that the kind of people who lived in HUD housing weren't "people of God" and we needed protection from them. I thought we were supposed to bring them into the church, not shut them out, and said so. Later, in private, I was told that women did not have a say in the matter. I continued to attend services, but that incident stayed with me. Over time, I felt that many churches preached fear to keep people in line, they often degraded women, and they dismissed anyone who wasn't *one of them.* Eventually I quit going altogether.

I thanked Garret for the information and closed the folder. He reached into the bag and pulled out several books, talking as he piled them in his lap.

"Here's some reading that might be helpful. *When God Doesn't Make Sense, Where Is God When It Hurts,* and *The Case for Faith.* Now I know you're plenty mad at God right now, but keep these and read them when you feel stronger." He dropped the books back in the bag.

"I've got plenty of faith," I said, tearing up.

"I know you do," Garret said. "Now you just got to believe that God knows what He's doing. And no matter what happens, you're safe in His love."

I stared at the bag of books. I'd already received a dozen such books, including one titled *How to Die*. I was so fucking mad that it went straight from the wrapping paper to the trashcan.

"My mother came to see me," I said. "She came and stood by my bed, and she's been dead for years." Garret lifted his eyebrows. Before he could say anything, I quickly told him about hearing the doctors and walking with my mother. For the sake of simplicity, I didn't mention that my grandparents had been there, too.

Garret dropped his eyes and studied his hands, then said, "That was the drugs, Barbara."

"No, it wasn't," I said loudly—loud enough to make me swimmy-headed. I settled against the pillow. "She was there. And I got up out of my body and went with her. I left and I came back."

Garret caught my eye and smiled. "It was the drugs."

"What about the spirit world?" I asked.

"That's not how spirit works."

"How do you *know*? How many spirits have you been in contact with?"

"I think I'm talking about the spirit and you're talking about ghosts," Garret said.

"God, you piss me off. I'm not talking about ghosts. She was there. And I knew all kinds of things."

"Like what?" Garret asked.

I tried to search my brain for something. I *did* know things while I was walking with her, things I couldn't possibly know. But what? I hadn't had much time to think about any of it because I was busy thinking that I might drop dead any minute. And now I couldn't remember.

"I could have gone with my mother," I said.

Garret looked skeptical.

The fact that I could have gone with my mother stayed with me; the rest had vanished like a giraffe made out of clouds. Still, I had been with my mother, and I knew that the barrier between her world and mine was not as impervious as I had imagined; it was there, like radio waves, just beyond my senses.

"You had a close call," Garret said. "You're frightened, and you have a right to be."

Suddenly exhausted, I relaxed and closed my eyes. Garret asked if he could say a prayer before he left and I nodded. He prayed for my quick recovery and for guidance for me. He worded it in a way that insinuated I wasn't thinking clearly, but I knew I was. I had gone somewhere else, some place very small or very large—and my mother and grandparents were there.

Garret left and Duane brought more drugs. I took them and closed my eyes again, but I wanted a few minutes to think before the drugs kicked in.

Garret had said I had had a *close call,* and I understood that. But now I questioned what *close call* really meant. This had not been my first one. In my tattered childhood, there were many. Once when I was a teenager, Dad didn't pick me up from my after-school baby-sitting job. The woman I worked for had plans that evening and refused to drive me home. She left me sitting on her steps, waiting for my father, who had by then settled onto a barstool for the night. It started to get dark and I took off for home on foot. Two men picked me up. As soon as the car began to move, I caught the familiar scent of stale cigarettes and whiskey. The hair on the back of my neck stood on end. Luckily I had climbed into the back seat and the men were in the front. I told them where I lived but they turned off onto the Birmingham highway and then onto an old country road, laughing as they talked of what they'd do to me. The driver slowed down, turned onto another road, and they put their heads together to finalize their plans. I dug into my purse and found an ink pen, one of those long straight Bic pens. Just the day before in gym class our physical education teacher had given us a self-defense lesson. She taught us how to use an ink pen as a weapon.

"Curl your fingers around the shaft and put your thumb on the top," Miss Scott had instructed. "Strike as if you're using a hammer."

The car slowed down to turn onto a dirt road and I stabbed the man on the passenger side. The pen dug into his left cheek. He yelled and grabbed his face, then reached back and snatched my right wrist, cursing loudly. The pen was in my left hand, and I repeatedly stabbed his arm as hard as I could. He screamed and the driver slammed on the brakes, throwing them forward, and thus breaking the hold on my arm. I opened the door and jumped out, and before they could gather their drunken wits, I got on my feet, ran across a field, and ducked under a barbwire fence.

Was it coincidence that our gym teacher had taught self-defense the very day before I desperately needed it?

And once, when Jason was about three years old, he stuck a cigarette lighter into the gas tank of John's motorcycle and lit it. I was absentmindedly sweeping the front porch as he played in the yard with Janet. Jason screamed as flames shot into the air, and I quickly snatched him off the bike and ran away from it. His eyelashes and eyebrows had been singed but otherwise he was unhurt. I burst into tears. He could have been blown to bits. I handed him to my mother and approached the motorcycle. Jason had somehow slapped the gas cap back into place and there was no sign of fire. I lifted the cap and peered into the tank. Small blue-green flames licked around the inside of the tank. I slapped the cap down and quickly moved everyone inside, certain that the bike would blow at any minute. It never did. Hours later, John came home and looked into the tank.

"It couldn't have been on fire, Barbara," he said in his doubting teenage-boy voice. "It would have blown like a stick of dynamite."

Yes, I thought. *How is it that it didn't?*

Thank you, God, I prayed, *for not letting anything happen to Jason, and for delivering me from those bad men; and for getting me through this surgery.* I opened my eyes and watched the birds flit around the feeder outside, and argued silently with myself. *Aren't those examples of God? Isn't that God? And what about my walk with Mother? Wasn't that God?* I put my hands on my torso and felt the metal staples under my shirt; my belly seemed hot, but I felt cold. Cold and thin. As if I'd been washed in hot water and had shrunk to practically nothing. Or to my very essence. No matter what—there was an awareness inside me, so unexplainable. *Isn't that God?* I argued. *God essence?* The drugs were catching up with me and I felt too confused to go on ruminating. A floating feeling washed over me and my eyes closed. *Dear God,* I prayed, *help me find my way.*

What We Will Call Nature

CIA WHITE

> When the world wearies
> And society ceases to satisfy
> There is always the garden.
> —Nineteenth-Century Homily, Cross-Stitched, Framed and Hung
> on a Bedroom Wall in the Late Years of the Twentieth Century

I made off from the landscape of my grown-up life in the middle of the night, when I was forty-three.

Early July, and a moat of fog was rising chest-high in pastures all around the house; cricket call went ratch-fitch as usual, volleying back and forth across the yard; under the long porch roof I met the scent of my tall Enchantment lilies, condensed in mist beaded on the bellied screen; and all of these familiars were tethers of a web I had to breast and tear, in walking out.

I drove off in a tunnel of headlights down one country lane after another, on a path with many turnings, like a branching intuition, leaving little Henry

County. My hands, legs, and chest got me along the thirty miles, first to the Interstate and then to the city, where there were bottle rockets popping on the street and the muffled booms of a big show at the river.

It wasn't like me—to veer off, to be abrupt, to be keen for once in the body's sufficient prudence. For years I'd stayed in place, subdued, bent to various intentions. Reading to the children from our illustrated book of myths, I saw my inner station reflected back to me by the picture of poor Psyche, head in hands, in the cell where Aphrodite set her to the task of sorting out the heap of jumbled beans and seeds. Perseverance Furthers,[1] I read and read, tutoring myself from the book of ancient oracles. And for years until the woodstove's heat dried it and the summer damp unglued it, a fortune-cookie slip was taped to the lamp on the little desk in a musty room I called my study and others called the parlor: "Patience is the cure for every ill."

It wasn't like me: I moved as if outside myself, wondering what I'd do next. So who was this, stone-deaf to conciliation and decorum, hardly dressed, and running barefoot from the house lit in only two windows? Who was this, with my own big hands, bare legs in shorts, wide neck—this ungovernable mare, prickling with new constellations of adrenaline and kicking off the traces? I recognized her anyway, and my diplomatic, skeptical, and matronly self—who had scrupulously kept her own counsel and disciplined her smallest impulse—surrendered to the plain ambitions of her body, and allowed herself to be delivered by this bolder being with her name.

I made off from a fortress, my retreat, my Edwardian novel of a house: the big white farmhouse, arrived in pieces from Sears, Roebuck at the river landing in 1907, and brought up to the ridge by wagons on an ox-cart road. In later years the house had suffered, during the decline of sons of sons of farmers, been kicked around, its gardens let to grow up in buckbush and motorcycle husks, until at last Miss Mena, a remnant in-law widow in the evaporating line of landowners, rescued it at auction, where her offer was delivered secondhand by a wily old country-courthouse lawyer in a trenchcoat and a porkpie hat.

Miss Mena sailed the neighborhood in her big boat of a car, in overalls and garden gloves, bidding the drawing of wagons into the yard to haul away rats' nests and trash, bidding the bushhogging of weeds, the scouring of dismay, and then the sale of the reborn house and three and one-half acres to the new family I was wife and mother in.

It was an old idea, this house, and also more (or less) than an idea: a loose tent conversant with the weather, where chimney swifts sometimes darted in the hallways, and plaster walls never finished making maps of fine cracks through winter, summer, winter.

I left my patched-on kitchen at the back—its caned rockers, goblets, antique platters, braided rugs, and bookshelves—where I was rooted at the sink, keeping my eye turned resolutely outward, toward worthy things in season: the long hill and water tower, the pasture creek rushing beyond its groove after heavy rain. The oak grove, which rattled oracularly in the fall, and was so deathly quiet and bare bones in the snow. The yellow horns of columbine against the black woodshed wall. Rain sweeping down in cloaks, thrown first across Miss Mena's neighboring fields and over Mister Harold's woodlot and black cattle, and then onto my gardens.

Down the road at F & F Feed and Coal, it was said that a Miss Velma, another eldress, long departed, had spent her last days bedfast in this house, locked by her son in a room upstairs, too old and sweet to stop him from taking down and selling the now-valuable domestic fittings of 1907: nickel-plated chandelier, crystal doorknobs, wrought-iron grate. She was said to have kept terrific gardens once, when her son was still a boy, and in my day I rediscovered her ambitions. In flowerbeds I dug, intending them to drape decorously like an embroidered hem beneath stoops and porches all around the house, I unearthed the wan surviving shoots of perennials she'd planted, this Miss Velma's old ideas of yarrow just here and peonies just there, cozied in against the white wall of the house. When I spaded up a border to define with bricks, I found her bricks half-crumbled five inches under sod, making just the subtle turn I'd planned myself, around the lilies of the valley. What I thought were my new brainstorms, lily starts mail ordered from Connecticut, went in beside her old original ones, and together they rose, staked to bamboo.

Miss Mena and I strolled satisfied among these revivals, praising the conspiring energies of Miss Velma and ourselves, and this, too, was company I left.

I left my half-acre vegetable garden (weedless, mulched, companion-planted), ringed with a hedge of honeysuckle and trumpet vine, ferny dillheads towering in the cucumbers. The expensive blue-perennial flowerbed in the shade, the asparagus patch, the purple clematis burgeoning over a white trellis, Moonbeam coreopsis, currant bushes, oakleaf hydrangea, jewelweed volunteers in the sawdust of the woodpile bed, borage, and rue.

I left the grapevines, golden raspberries, heirloom apple trees I planted; the bleeding heart, white daffodils, rhubarb. The dwarf cherry tree, the mint bog at the creek, porch swing, pickle crocks, the murmuring of clean white bantam hens foraging in the shade of redbud trees. The contemplation of tin roof, cold chimney, and clouds trailing away, through the stroking fronds of a walnut tree. The rope swing hung from a ragged limb, where a big rat snake periodically rubbed off its papery skin, and left it flying like a banner.

I left behind the landmarks of my walks off the county road, where in untended places the country reel of change and return was danced for me, a city girl. I left a large investment of attention, a steady work to root and make familiar knowledge, living in one peaceful place for a long time. A speechless time, still it was the heyday of my eyes: the laying open by winter of the thicket at the river, the reconcealment of stacks of stranded trash and driftwood by midsummer vines, the crosshatched windstrokes on the cold pond. The appearance of yellow plums on a tree I'd once driven home from the nursery, with its leafless head out the window and its rootball seatbelted in. I'd seen that tree through drought; I'd prayed against the borer.

I left behind the locations of my earnest labor: big black tobacco barns I helped to fill to the rafters, handing up the gummy skirts of plants I helped to cut and spear in long, hot patches. Wringer washer on the back porch, laundry line between two trees, ten stooped steps uphill on a slope you could almost call a cliff. The cairn of flagstones where I did my walnut work.

Those walnuts were prodigious, everybody said so, the green hulls as big as hedge apples or cannonballs, and one winter I achieved a worm-free feedsack full and perched there in the afternoons, in an overcoat and workboots, crushing stony walnuts with a brick, picking out with a nail two wing-shaped meats from each shell, nutmeats so large it took only half a dozen to make a teacake. Which teacake I surely did make. Until Easter of that year my fingers were walnut-black in every crease.

Now I keep sensations of that time, archived in the body—the thundering of walnut hulls landing on the tin roof in the fall; the sharp limey smell of their rinds crumbling in the grass; the Holy-Land fans of leaves—and laid among them is the history of my disappointed innocence, now named humbly, but not simply, only Walnut.

I left my books: my Christian apologetics, my annotated Milton, my Jane Austens, my sacred geometries, my autographed copies, and forty-six gold-embossed volumes of *The Great Books,* full of silverfish, in a bookcase on the open landing.

I left my clothes, my silk shirtwaists and calico sundresses. I left my smooth tables, my chintz-covered chairs, the long fringed muslin curtains, the six-foot lilies at the sitting room window.

I left my root cellar, with its villages of green beans, gooseberry jam, homemade marinara sauce, sauerkraut, and its wilderness corners where potatoes grew long snarls of tangled white sprouts trying to root in the dust.

I left behind the single grave of stillborn twin daughters, in a small-town cemetery on a hillside four rural counties north. Their names are marked there on a small flat stone in coarse grass shaded by black walnut trees.

I left my little country church, its muted sisterhood of tough old women and mothers of the very young; the iron belltower in a weedy lot; the goats brought in to crop the antique graveyard clean, and the bad boys who let them out at midnight to clatter down the road to town. The whirring of fans and crickets in summer. The trembling hymns. The coal stove in winter. The succession of baffled seminarian pastors. The four farmer-deacons on tiptoes, whispering, pouring grape juice so carefully into fifty glass thimbles in the damp basement kitchen.

I left my marriage of twenty years.

I left my companions—the women I read books with, gossiped on the phone with, deplored the modern world with, organized bazaars and birthday parties with, jitterbugged at New Year's with, the armchairs piled with our little girls in smocked dresses, watching us good mothers reel each other out and in. To see us dance amazed them; it didn't happen often. But if it was my house where the party was (and if there was a party, that was where it was), and if the men self-selected their own society and took up all the chairs (and if the men were there, they did), then we women would drift aside, backing into the hallway, and dance, one night a year.

In the nine thousand other hours of the year, we good mothers had closed our own childhoods tight, and our adulthoods we meant to set as sober good examples, especially to our husbands. Flanked by toddler bodyguards, we stood restless in hallways and on porches, engrossed in the protective disciplines.

I brought with me—certainly, I brought my children with me. I lifted my long-legged son from his bed in a room full of flags, and carried him through the darkened farmhouse and across the porch, settled him in the passenger seat, closed the car doors methodically and silently. Like a single towhee singing in a tree that night, he made cheerful small talk about the setting moon, asking me no questions. My daughter was sleeping in a tent in the pine woods two hundred miles away at Girl Scout camp, but she, too, was my company; in spirit I caught her up.

And at last I left behind a certain custom of my grown-up mind, a fastidious, ironic timbre. For a long time it had mastered me, going straight to work on native feeling, pecking away its patterns of holes where the wine leaked out.

In the regime of a persnickety voice, a body finds counsel otherwise, and I found mine in trees I knew as interceding deities or mistresses, inviting my familiarity.

Hungry for enactments of transformation outside my window, for the yielding of narrow forms to an irresistible ripening, I sent my unexpressed ardor into theirs, across mown fields.

Off duty, I studied their erotic model, admired for dear life the venturesome passions of newly knuckled twigs, of roots groping the rock shelf, nosing for the door to deeper earth. I was consoled by their large bodies, by their various tempestuous expressions in confinement: the thrashing of sugar maple branches in the dry gusts before a storm; the bone-white bark of bare sycamores grouped along the frozen creek. The broken old pear tree at the far end of the orchard, which threw to the ground in her last summer bushel after bushel, a wild finale of perfect fruit. The stately threesome of shagbark hickories outside the bedroom windows, especially on those days in spring when the tight pods of their leafbuds split, and from each dropped furled leaves, like clenched hands blooming into fingers.

Householders complained about a mess of windfall apples, drawing wasps and tracked inside, or of sycamore leaves, big and brown as tattered grocery sacks, littering a clipped yard; I turned away, incensed.

In the county park, under a young ash tree by the side of a muddy lake where my children were running to the shallows and back again to me with news of floppy handstands and mud castles, I used to sit alone, stiffnecked, on the lookout for malicious currents or bees in the clover grass. But for just a minute I lay down, one hand on an ankle-like knob of root, content to be explored by ants, looking up through stairstep branches, and let my body feel its own haphazard gist of glee. I whispered reckless scraps of French; English was too scrupulous.

Copine, ma vieille . . . , I made it up, lovetalk to a tree or to the supple spirit it embodied, before the supervising voice took note, and I sat bolt upright, peering out to the green, deep, middle of the lake, recalled again to vigilance. Precisely folding up the picnic sacks, I rebuffed what seemed the taproot of unrighteousness, this mischief muscling up in me.

You might have visited me there in the country, on your way to California or Manhattan. You might have been curious about the local culture. If you had come to visit, to sit on the porch with a glass of wine and watch the purple martins gather in their house on a high pole in the middle of the garden, you would have seen a woman apparently cured of her passions and skeptical about yours, comfortable in an old-fashioned order, serving a prodigious lunch at a long table with a centerpiece of nodding local wildflowers and zinnias. There would have been authoritative conversation among the men, and their lounging satisfied. I would have avoided your eye, and snatched away the salad plates. You might have wondered about that, later, in the car on the way to the airport, in the same hour that I finished cleaning up from lunch, and walked down a mown path to pick apples in the orchard and reconsider in private the mane of your hair.

I worried that I might be like the worshippers of Baal or Sappho's acolytes. I put on weight, and drew protective circles of Lenten silence around my babies. Stooping to tuck potato parings under leaves of transplants, I was devoted to a cloistered order, to the perfect plumb of clothespins on a line, while I entertained a tower-chamber full of suspicious examiners in the mind.

Their register is certain, male, rich with erudition, style. Harried by the private noise of them, I flopped clumsily, between extremes of grandiosity and shame.

("And just who do we think we are?" asked a sharp voice, the master of novices, a stringent one. "H. D. Thoreau?")

(With drawling irony: "Generally, when persons . . . quote *find* themselves unquote . . . it is to everyone else's eternal regret.")

These voices jealously administer the treasury of all ambitious nouns (*Nature, Virtue, History*). They take the high road in both lanes, assigning governed postures at the crossways, splitting hairs to set me straight.

They supervise feeling, that unruly slattern, and direct my attention to something graver and less impolitic: to a succession of stiff silhouettes, the saturnine stewards of civilization, my patrons and gallants, the holders of the reins of syntax, the rattlers of ice cubes in tumblers of good scotch, the brayers and by-Godders, the last few friends of reason, by whose thoughts we are saved from ourselves. For them the body is low housing.

I left behind, on a shelf below the antique butter churn, my collection of old gardening books. Dark green or navy blue, with titles in gold curlicues embossed along the spines, they contained quaint concoctions for antidotes to blights on roses, plans for arbors, or the espaliering of quince.

Among these manuals was a less practical old book. Found at a farm sale for a dollar, along with a mattock and a sieve, it was an anonymous contemplative diary, entitled *The Solitary Summer,* its publication undatable except by the inscription of a onetime reader, on the flyleaf in faded ornate penmanship: Mrs. Joshua P. Honeycutt, Louisa, Kentucky, Christmas, 1901.

The unnamed author was a gentlewoman, describing country life in a summer she began daringly, by announcing her desire to spend time entirely alone. It was a wish her husband (whom she calls throughout "The Man of Wrath") grudgingly half-granted: much of the three months was spent as usual, in his cautionary purview, though he was also apt on rainy afternoons to mistake her for a cushion in the darkened parlor.

She performed her customary duties—doling out sausages from the larder, presiding over lunch and dinner, declining to fire the unsatisfactory cook just yet, enduring lengthy visits by dour Lutheran ministers and by young officers barracked in the village, persisting in her wake from room to room, going on about the histories of their regiments—but she also took her own pleasure, by firm intention, in snatches when she could. She writes about stealing out at three in the morning to walk in her meandering gardens, and creeping back to bed relieved to have found among white rocket-flowers her "real and natural self"; about going alone with a book into patches of lupines, or to an unhygienic frogpond, with a picnic of radishes and her little girls, whom she plucked away from the catechizing business of their schoolmaster.

She practiced unconventional gardening, forgiving and experimental, most ambitious in wild groves at the far back of the house: she was disdainful of grand fronts, with ubiquitous "carpet-bedding and glass balls on pedestals."

The loveliest garden I know is spoilt to my thinking by the impossibility of getting out of sight of the house, which stares down at you, Argus-eyed and unblinking, into whatever corner you may shuffle. . . . [T]he borders [are] exquisite examples of taste, the turf so faultless that you hardly like to walk on it for fear of making it dusty, and the whole quite uninhabitable for people of my solitary tendencies, because, go where you will, you are overlooked.

"Go where you will, you are overlooked." I lingered there, musing at the double entendre. To be continually "overlooked"—spied upon from up above; or mistaken for a cushion.

She was a furtive ecstatic, my anonymous diarist, carried away by the plantation of Madonna lilies, "so chaste in their appearance, so voluptuous in their smell." A bunch of cowslips she "kissed and kissed again . . . because of all the kisses in the world there is none other so exquisite."

She was afraid she might be taken for "a person who rhapsodizes." Though in the mornings alone she felt "almost a poet and . . . wholly a joyous animal," she trudged back reluctantly at luncheon time to the order of the house, to "cutlets and . . . revengeful sweet things," where she kept her sensory adventures to herself.

> I generally succeed in keeping quiet; but sometimes even now, after years of study in the art of holding my tongue, some stray fragment of what I feel does occasionally come out, and then I am at once pulled up and brought back to my senses by the well-known cold stare of utter incomprehension.

Long ago she gave up the hope of sympathetic company. "How is it that you should feel so vastly superior?" she asked unnamed persons in her thought.

She went to pains to conceal the precise region of her home. She scolded herself in a sly voice for her unauthorized private opinions of Goethe and Thoreau. She sidled in the nick of time from contention into irony, or some new winsome observation; from lapses into melancholy, she purposefully uprighted herself, bedazzling herself back into a teetering contentment by means of a silver birch growing in a bank of wild azaleas, at the isolated far end of a walk.

She was a clever woman of her time, in short, her track well camouflaged, and thereby something of a mystery—but maybe much more mysterious, I thought, to those she lived among, than to Mrs. J. P. Honeycutt, 1901, perhaps, and me.

We women at the sink conspired with ineffable smiles, news of our old disappointments. A man's voice broke in, and we suddenly ungrouped, surprised, our faces falsely clearing.

Then, overheard, we talked round and round: half-draped judgments, worryworry over others' errors, daily matter-of-facts in prospect and retrospect and back again, talk of what we thawed and what we baked, for whom, and took it when. In this atmosphere, the lords of household smiled, comfortable and comforted while we were talking all at once—like birdsong, an impersonal and uninflected line, a perseverance to warble, around the well-defined edges of men's stories, illuminating, but not alighting.

Or we hushed, and each kept her own sublime counsel. Our gazes fell away, incurious, unreadable. We might have looked almost beatified, like portrait subjects of great men—shawled women silent in the early evening, cutting roses on a garden path or stacking apples in our aprons.

We did not reach into the company of feasters. We declined to take up room in the rooms whose comforts we sustained. A woman living here did not lean in with her singular peculiar person, with her elbows on the common table, betraying an intent purpose of narration, and by narration, connection. She did not begin with, "This is what I know. . . ."

And if, helplessly inspired, we did (a time or two) begin like that, something in the atmosphere would set upon the story from the start: the opening cadence would sound somehow hapless and contrary, landing across the grain in conversation; a civil silence would sift over what we'd said, and the men would look away forbearingly, out the window or at their plates.

Better not to impose, to stride, or speak, though we half-knew what we meant to say. The voice was firm: This ambition does not become you. This is not important, direct speech of the body.

To step out is abandonment. In an eighteenth-century engraving, a woman (somber face, hair coiled in a pearled snood) lifts the heavy housing of her brocade skirt with both hands, and imposes one small black-booted foot deliberately into a stream. Reading her assuredly, the museum placard translates a dire iconography: here we see depicted female debauch, betrayal of the moral to the sensual.

The tumbling stream teems with rank contagion; experts have so warned us.

The intricately folded fields I left, the morning glories on stone fences, were no enemies of mine, but that night I spurned them just the same. The turning of the key in the ignition of the car was an outright reply, a creaturely roar, and with it I turned, too, baring my eyeteeth.

I left to step out of an old topiary way, and let my native being be.

It was late, but not too late, to embrace my lover and meet my match, in a woman.

I left in order to ripen willy-nilly as I am, not rearranged like an espaliered bough.

I've admired the erect walk of women carrying full baskets on their heads, who never stumble and spill, and I've thought to walk it, too, but now was time to drive like mad, thinking not a thing but left, right, left, with fog shredding in the low-beams and mending behind me.

The Superior Man[2] makes no such precipitous moves as I did, sweeping detail aside, spraying dust. The Superior Man moves with a sturdy step across thresholds when and as they come. From his youth he stands up straight and counsels with the company of peers.

In nature the Superior Man reads ideograms that dignify an arrangement in which he has authority, freedom of movement, and no reason to make unseemly haste, or mutiny.

On these and other plainer grounds, I was not the Superior Man.

The voice, a linguist in its spare time, reminds me of kindred words: *perverse, perversion.* The Latin root *vers* means a "turning"; the Latinate prefix *per*, "thoroughly." To be perverse is to turn thoroughly against fundamental law. Perversions are the domestic consequence—lamentable indulgences by persons who go to swim against the current: against Nature.

Or against what we will call Nature. (In this dominion, Nature's productions are read selectively.) "Your yearning shall be for your husband," Jehovah curses Eve, hallowing the peculiar way our characters would be honed against a grindstone, "yet he will lord it over you."[3]

But I mean to tell my own *true* perverse adventures. Among the conscientious words in the treasury of the voice, this one—true—to my surprise came out tactile, mine to bring from my pocket homely as a buckeye, a skate key, a locust bean, like the lowly object at the bottom of the wayfarer's pack in a fairy tale.

(*"Truth!"* huffs the voice. Like Pilate, incredulous of philosophy in the hands of colonials: "What is *'truth'*?")

Just the same, I can be plain. The impressive voice is tireless and withering, but a body can turn thoroughly, and walk away beyond its ken, into numinous gritty worlds, into sound perches of solitude. A mind can put aside imperious evaluations of the green text; a mind can defer to the body, the disheveled stranger surprising the assembly of feasters, and allow the body its ranging story.

In that story, an unstudied gist remains intact, a problematical bliss, kept somehow competent and hardy. The story's original landscapes lie behind the nutlike monosyllables of common nouns—milk, rain, stream, plum—and are preserved in the senses in mysterious concentrations, by the way a ferocious fume of memory will rise from the bruising of a warted leaf. Left to its own mere lore, the body locates its task and honor of participation, in the dark room behind the breastbone, where we keep the plainest old appetite for touch.

Now I'm working in a screened second-story porch at the back of a house in a new leafy neighborhood, in a small city on a big river, in a state still governed jealously by sons of sons. This house where I landed looks onto an avenue shaded by tall maples. At one end of the street, three blocks away, is a bronze town-father on a pacing horse in boxwood and impatiens. Four blocks the other way is an old landscaped cemetery for Confederate dead and the first families of the city. I walk there, for the muscular chestnut trees, the peonies, the weathered lambs and angels of nineteenth-century children's graves.

I use the back-alley entrance to this city house, past the manna-fall of Styrofoam in pokebushes and tansyweed, between the rows of chainlink fence fuzzied with mimosa sprouts, up the covered stairwell to the high back porch.

From the porch, an old saucer magnolia in the neighbor's yard is eye level with me. In spring before it leafs, it flowers, gigantically erotic with pink cones falling open. From the windows I salute it often. I look down also on a snarled mock orange bush, too tall, hilarious, akimbo. There is no sublime form to prune it to.

("Ah. How convenient," says the supervising voice. "Yes. Now, *this* has been known as the Pathetic Fallacy. One ascribes to the natural world some little human feeling. One presumes a sentimental association with the primrose.")

I storm across the slanted floor of my perch ("—an error pathetic in *both* senses of the word—") to the bookshelf, and yank out Margaret Drabble's *Oxford Companion to English Literature:* the Pathetic Fallacy, Ruskin's term, bawling out Wordsworth. Same old boys' brawl about the perimeters of virtue. Ah yourself, I say.

("You shall have no gods except me." You shall not pray to bushes.)

(I might pray to bushes: Mimosa, buckeye, redwood-shagbark, laurel, maple, and ash.)

On this sloping porch, I have other indispensable works of reference: a shopping bag full of family photographs, an oval watercolor of my childhood home (maples, rhododendrons, mimosa with a summer show of tufted pink cockades; many gabled shuttered windows, like blindered eyes), and the big tree presently inclining her head toward me.

I have a teetering stack of my own journals, where I find titanic garden plans, sketches of quilt designs, notes on the needs of difficult plants and difficult people, menus for High Teas, thoughtful elaborations of various scriptures. The superintending voice has left a dense record of its good works, with its avuncular suggestions, its henceforths and forthwiths—but here and there, there are these resounding lapses: dreams to shock a body awake, blunt monologues suspended in mid-sentence, and the names of women I've desired in secret, encoding in imagination what I declined on earth.

Like a crumb path suddenly plain in a clearing, I find these names and presences. I can speak of them now, my companions in imagined exodus to ragged woods or sunstruck rooms, where our vocabulary is tolerant of what is lax, and we are kindred serenities, limb on limb.

With one lifetime all askew in folders, I can go back now, to look into what I had thought to put aside. A photograph of myself at ten, at the garden gate, chin in hand. I see even there and then the wayward way I've taken now, stubborn like a whorl in wood. And earlier, in this one: the sharp elbows of a five-year-old, plunked down on a little desktop, are parts of me I would come to be obliged to use abruptly, to clear a path. And surely here is an eccentric creature, standing at the fenced Potomac River at seventeen, self-concealing, metal-mouthed, precocious studier of Milton and Maryell, in the least defiant of costumes, trying not to grin or scowl, but braced against the breeze in a certain sturdy way. I can see determination here, and the gathering of a "flood that can't be folded / And put inside a drawer."[4] I can see mutiny coming up—not soon, but soon enough.

From girlhood we aspired, informed in our bones for the dance we rarely danced, a long intrepid unwrapping of the treasure of creaturehood. But another voice broke in, calling us to take its higher road, to admire its arranging zeal with regard to nature and spirit, weed and flower, sheep and goat, genre and form. Indeed some of us took refuge when and where we were allowed to range, in silent retreat and alone, in woods and gardens we didn't own, in mornings and evenings beyond the tall schoolmaster's eye.

But now we make outright for the door, and for wholesome company—for light and air, like tendrils in a cellar. Who cares which strand is form and which is genre? One is teeth, and one is tongue, and together they collaborate to speak, they shout and sing.

My son is now fourteen. For reasons of his own, his hair is dyed a mossy green. Along the city boulevard of smoothie-stands and Twelve-Step bookstores and neo-Christian coffeehouses which come and go, he runs the bristling gauntlet of the world, in shade of big embattled maples. My daughter, sixteen, collects herself and all she sees, mysteriously behind the veil of her hair. Grown very tall, she experiments with a variety of bold, enormous hats, flowing robes in fire colors, big patchwork wingtip shoes; she writes.

We drive in the country, my lover and I, with the windows rolled down. The Ohio River, in flood, tumbles downstream as we go up. Bridged, riprapped, bobbing hapless drift (Clorox bottles, rags, knots of wire fence), the river is roaring with authority, heaving up an iron breast where no little lives can safely make their own ways. But on this road native dogwood and mimosa reach out from the edge of the woods through low brambles, and emerge in waving layers, never still, and by no means hostile to what we will call our natures.

Notes

1. "Perseverance Furthers" is a piece of advice frequently repeated in the I Ching, the book of Taoist oracles.

2. The Superior Man is the model of stewardship and leadership in the I Ching.

3. These words of Yahweh are quoted from the New Jerusalem translation of the Bible (1966 ed.).

4. The quoted lines are Emily Dickinson's.

Contributors

MITZI ADAMS is a solar scientist for NASA's Marshall Space Flight Center, now housed in the National Space Sciences and Technology Center in Huntsville, Alabama. Born in Atlanta, Georgia, she graduated from Georgia State University with a B.S. in physics and earned the M.S. degree (also in physics) from The University of Alabama in Huntsville. An avid world traveler, she also explores caves, sometimes under water, and is both a runner and a tap dancer. As a teenager, she thought about becoming an astronaut but "decided that I didn't really want to be an astronaut . . . and am very happy in my profession, solar astronomer." Her research focuses on the magnetic fields associated with sunspots and on solar coronal features. She writes of her cave diving: "Although not an astronaut, I'm still an explorer. I frequently explore caves in the north Alabama area and sometimes, I even explore caves under the water. Cave diving is a very, very dangerous sport, but I find the underwater world that I visit is fascinating and enticing. Very few other humans have visited some of the caves. Others are quite popular and see traffic each weekend. But all are very beautiful. I love to watch air bubbles collect on the ceiling; they look like gems. The sweep of the lights on the cave walls illuminates areas that may not have seen light for thousands or millions or years. In some caves, those that flooded long after the caves formed, we see stalactites and stalagmites, just like in dry caves. And because the water is so clear, swimming twenty or thirty feet off the cave bottom almost seems like we're hovering in air."

MARILOU AWIAKTA is a poet, storyteller, and essayist. She grew up in Oak Ridge, Tennessee, a federal center for nuclear research. Awiakta's unique weaving of her Cherokee and Appalachian heritages with science has brought national and international recognition, beginning in the early 1980s, when the U.S. Information Agency chose her first two books, *Abiding Appalachia: Where Mountain and Atom Meet* (poetry) and *Rising Fawn and the Fire Mystery* (novella), for the global tour of its cultural centers.

Since its publication in 1993, her nonfiction book, *Selu: Seeking the Corn Mother's Wisdom,* has been widely studied in colleges and universities. *Selu* applies the American Indian concept of respect for the web of life to contemporary issues. It was a Quality Paperback Book Club Selection (1994) and the audio version was nominated for a Grammy Award in 1996. Quotes from *Selu* are engraved in the Fine Arts Walkway at UCLA, Riverside, and the Riverwall of the Bicentennial Capitol Mall in Nashville, Tennessee.

Awiakta has a B.A. from the University of Tennessee, 1958. Her life and work are profiled in the *Oxford American Companion to Women's Writing in the U.S.* Honors include awards for "Distinguished Tennessee Writer" (1989), "Educational Service to Appalachia" (Carson Newman College, 1999), "Appalachian Writer 2000" (Shepherd College), "Meritorious Service to American Indian People" (Northeastern State University of Oklahoma, 1999), and an honorary "Doctorate in Humane Letters" from Albion College in Michigan. Awiakta says, "The sustaining root of my life has been my husband, Paul, our three children, four grandchildren, and 'the Spirit that binds the universe as one.'"

AMY BLACKMARR is an award-winning Georgia author who became a familiar public radio voice when she left her Kansas paralegal business to move into her grandfather's fishing shack in south Georgia, where she grew up, and turn to writing full-time. Her acclaimed collections of personal essays relate wrenching tales of her experiences with the natural world while living in rustic hideouts tucked far back in the woods. She was a Madison A. & Lila Self Fellow at the University of Kansas, holds a Ph.D. in English, and has been a popular speaker for more than ten years on the subject of the personal essay and the relationship between the natural world and the creative life. She is the author of *Above the Fall Line: The Trail from White Pine Cabin* (Mercer U.P., 2003), named in 2008 by the Georgia Center for the Book to its list of "Top-25 Books All Georgians Should Read"; *Going to Ground: Simple Life on a Georgia Pond* (Viking 1997, Penguin 1998, Mercer U.P., 2003), named in 2005 by the Georgia Center for the Book to its list of "Top-25 Books All Georgians Should Read"; and *House of Steps: Finding the Path Home* (Viking 1999). In 2004, she was the winner of the Georgia Author of the Year (Essay Division) from the Georgia Writers Association for *Above the Fall Line: The Trail from White Pine Cabin* (Mercer U.P., 2003).

MARSHALL CHAPMAN (www.tallgirl.com) is an American singer-songwriter. Over the years, she has recorded twelve critically acclaimed albums, and her songs have been recorded by everybody from Jimmy Buffett and Emmylou Harris to Joe Cocker and Irma Thomas. Her current CD, *Big Lonesome*, was named "Best Country/Roots Album of 2010" by the *Philadelphia Inquirer.* (*Paste Magazine* called it "her masterpiece.") Her first book, *Goodbye, Little Rock and Roller,* was a SIBA Book Award finalist (2004), and her most recent book, *They Came to Nashville,* is a SIBA Book Award nominee (2011). Marshall has written commentary for *The Bob Edwards Show* and is currently a contributing editor to *Garden & Gun* and *Nashville Arts Magazine*. In addition to her recording and writing careers, in 2011 she starred in her first motion picture, playing Gwyneth Paltrow's road manager in *Country Strong*. A lapsed Presbyterian, Marshall lives in Nashville with her husband, Chris Fletcher.

SUSAN CUSHMAN'S feature-length piece, "Icons Will Save the World," was published in *First Things: The Journal of Religion, Culture and Public Life*. Her essay, "Blocked," was a finalist in the Santa Fe Writers Project Literary Awards, and was published in *sfwp Journal*. Susan's story of her Korean son's search for his birth mother, "The Other Woman," appeared in *Mom Writers Literary Magazine*. A native of Jackson, Mississippi, Susan's efforts to embrace her cultural roots while exploring an unconventional spiritual path are reflected in essays such as "myPod," "Burying Saint Joseph," and "Super-Sized Enlightenment," which were all published in *skirt! Magazine*. Susan was director of the 2011 Memphis Creative Nonfiction Workshop, codirector of the 2010 Oxford Creative Nonfiction Conference (Oxford, Mississippi), and a panelist at the 2009 Southern Women Writers Conference (Berry College, Rome, Georgia). She lives in Memphis, where she is currently working on a novel and a nonfiction book about the benefits of memorizing poetry while writing prose. She paints Byzantine-style icons with egg tempera and gold leaf. She blogs at http://wwwpenandpalette-susancushman.blogspot.com/, is a regular guest blogger for Jane Friedman's *Writer's Digest* blog, "There Are No Rules," and is also a regular on the Southern Author's Blog, "A Good Blog is Hard to Find."

BETH ANN FENNELLY directs the MFA Program at Ole Miss and lives in Oxford with her husband and three children. She has won grants from the N.E.A., the MS Arts Commission, and United States Artists. Her work has three times been included in *The Best American Poetry* series. Fennelly has published three full-length poetry books. Her first, *Open House,* won The 2001 *Kenyon Review* Prize and the Great Lakes College Association New Writers Award, and was a Book Sense Top Ten Poetry Pick. It was reissued by W. W. Norton in 2009. Her second book, *Tender Hooks,* and her third, *Unmentionables,* were published by W. W. Norton in 2004 and 2008. She has also published a book of nonfiction, *Great with Child,* in 2006, with Norton. As a Contributing Editor to *The Oxford American,* she frequently writes essays on Southern food, music, and books.

CONNIE MAY FOWLER is an award-winning author of six novels and a memoir. Her novels include *How Clarissa Burden Learned to Fly, Sugar Cage, River of Hidden Dreams, The Problem with Murmur Lee, Remembering Blue*—recipient of the Chautauqua South Literary Award—and *Before Women Had Wings*—recipient of the 1996 Southern Book Critics Circle Award and the Francis Buck Award from the League of American Pen Women. Connie adapted *Before Women Had Wings* for Oprah Winfrey. The result was an Emmy-winning film starring Ms. Winfrey and Ellen Barkin. In 2002, she published *When Katie Wakes,* a memoir that explores her descent and escape from an abusive relationship. Her work has been translated into eighteen languages and is published worldwide. Her essays have been published in *The New York Times, The London Times,* the *International Herald Tribune, The Japan Times, Oxford American, Best Life,* and elsewhere. She is currently working on her next project, an environmental memoir that explores the psychological and spiritual effects of the BP oil disaster on everyday life along the northern Gulf of Mexico coast. She serves on the faculty of The Afghan Women's Writing Project and teaches in the Vermont College of Fine Art's low residency creative writing MFA program.

MARGARET GIBSON is the author of ten books of poems and one prose memoir. Louisiana University Press has published her poetry, including *Second Nature* in 2010. *Long Walks in the Afternoon* was a Lamont Selection in 1982, *Memories of the Future* the cowinner of the Melville Cane Award in 1986. *The Vigil* was a Finalist for the National Book Award in Poetry in 1993. *Icon and Evidence* was a Finalist for the Virginia Center for the Book Award and the Connecticut Center for the Book Award in 2002, and *Autumn Grasses* was a Finalist in 2004 for the Connecticut Center for the Book Award, an award *One Body* won in 2008. Her memoir, *The Prodigal Daughter,* was published by University of Missouri Press in 2008, and was a Finalist for the Connecticut Book Award in Memoir and Biography in 2009. Margaret Gibson lives in Preston, Connecticut.

JENNIFER HORNE is the author of *Bottle Tree: Poems* (WordTech, 2010), the editor of *Working the Dirt: An Anthology of Southern Poets* (NewSouth Books, 2003), and coeditor, with Wendy Reed, of *All Out of Faith: Southern Women on Spirituality* (University of Alabama Press, 2006). Horne has received fellowships from the Alabama State Council on the Arts and the Seaside Institute. She grew up in Arkansas and has lived in Alabama since 1986. She holds a B.A. in the Humanities from Hendrix College, and an M.A. in English, an M.F.A. in Creative Writing, and an M.A. in Community Counseling, all from The University of Alabama. Horne currently teaches in The University of Alabama Honors College and serves as poetry book reviews editor for *First Draft Reviews Online.*

RHETA GRIMSLEY JOHNSON has covered the South for over three decades as a newspaper reporter and columnist. She writes about ordinary but fascinating people, mining for universal meaning in individual stories. In past reporting for United Press International, *The Commercial Appeal* of Memphis, the *Atlanta Journal Constitution* and a number of other regional newspapers, Johnson has won national awards. They include the Ernie Pyle Memorial Award for human interest reporting (1983), the Headliner Award for commentary (1985), and the American Society of Newspaper Editors' Distinguished Writing Award for commentary (1982). In 1986, she was inducted into the Scripps Howard Newspapers Editorial Hall of Fame. In 1991, Johnson was one of three finalists for the Pulitzer Prize for commentary. Syndicated today by King Features of New York, Johnson's column appears in about fifty papers nationwide. She is the author of several books, including *Enchanted Evening Barbie and the Second Coming* (2010), *Poor Man's Provence: Finding Myself in Cajun Louisiana* (2008), *America's Faces* (1987), and *Good Grief: The Story of Charles M. Schulz* (1989). In 2000, she wrote the text for a book of photographs entitled *Georgia*. A native of Colquitt, Georgia, Johnson grew up in Montgomery, Alabama, studied journalism at Auburn University, and has lived and worked in the South all of her career. She was married to the late journalism professor Don Grierson. In December 2010, Johnson married retired Auburn University history professor Hines Hall.

MARY KARR is an award-winning poet and best-selling memoirist. She is the author of *Lit,* the long-awaited sequel to her critically acclaimed and *New York Times* best-selling memoirs *The Liars' Club* and *Cherry.* A born raconteur, she brings to her lectures and talks the same wit, irreverence, joy, and sorrow found in her poetry and prose. Karr welcomes conversation with her audience and she is known for her spirited, lively, and engaging Q&A sessions. Her poetry grants include The Whiting Writer's Award, an NEA, a Radcliffe Bunting Fellowship, and a Guggenheim. She has won prizes from Best American Poetry as well as Pushcart Prizes for both poetry and essays. Her four volumes of poetry are *Sinners Welcome* (HarperCollins, 2006), *Viper Rum* (Penguin, 1998), *The Devil's Tour* (New Directions, 1993), and *Abacus* (Carnegie Mellon, 1986). Her work appears in such magazines as *The New Yorker, The Atlantic, Poetry,* and *Parnassus.* Karr is the Jesse Truesdell Peck Professor of Literature at Syracuse University and was the weekly poetry editor for the *Washington Post Book World*'s "Poet's Choice" column, a position canonized by Bob Hass, Ed Hirsch, and Rita Dove. She lives in Syracuse, New York, and New York City.

DEBRA MOFFITT is a world traveler and author of *Awake in the World: 108 Ways to Live a Divinely Inspired Life* (Llewellyn Worldwide, 2011). She teaches workshops on spirituality and writing at the Sophia Institute and other venues in the United States and Europe. Her mind/body/spirit articles, essays, and stories appear in publications around the globe and were broadcast by BBC World Services Radio. Visit her online at: *www.debramoffitt.com.*

BARBARA ROBINETTE MOSS earned a BFA from Ringling School of Art & Design in Sarasota, Florida, and an MFA from Drake University in Des Moines, Iowa. She was the 1996 winner of the Gold Medal for Personal Essay in the William Faulkner Creative Writing Contest, and the author of the books *Change Me into Zeus's Daughter* and *Fierce: A Memoir.* She was also an accomplished artist whose work appeared in over one hundred juried exhibitions. She died in 2009.

BRENDA MARIE OSBEY is an author of poetry and of prose nonfiction in English and French. The first peer-selected poet laureate of Louisiana (2005–2007), Osbey is a native New Orleanian and currently teaches at Louisiana State University.

WENDY REED, Ph.D., writes, produces, teaches, and directs at The University of Alabama Center for Public Television and Radio. She has received two Regional Emmys for her work with *Discovering Alabama* and also directs/produces the series *Bookmark* along with documentaries. She received fellowships from the Alabama State Council on the Arts and the Seaside Institute. She is coeditor, with Jennifer Horne, of *All Out of Faith: Southern Women on Spirituality* (University of Alabama Press, 2006). Her next book, *An Accidental Memoir: How I Killed Someone and Other Stories* (NewSouth Books), includes memoir among fiction and essays.

VALERIE REISS is a writer, editor, blogger, and certified yoga instructor in Brooklyn, New York. Her work has appeared in *The New York Times, Newsweek, Women's Health, Natural Health, Yoga Journal, Beliefnet,* and *Vegetarian Times.* She served as Holistic Living & Blogs Editor at *Beliefnet.com,* a National Magazine Award–winning website covering spirituality, where she also cowrote Beliefnet's *Fresh Living* blog. She was previously Articles Editor at *Breathe,* a yoga-inspired lifestyle magazine. A native New Yorker, Valerie has an M.S. from Columbia University's Graduate School of Journalism and a B.A. from Beloit College in Creative Writing and Women's Studies.

STELLA SUBERMAN was born and raised in Union City, Tennessee, the setting of her first memoir, *The Jew Store* (Algonquin Books, 1998). She spent her teen years in Miami Beach, Florida, attended the University of Miami and Florida State College for Women, and after marriage, spent twenty years in North Carolina, where she was the publications chief for the North Carolina Museum of Art and a book reviewer for the *Raleigh News and Observer.* She returned to Florida in 1966 as the administrative director of the University of Miami's Lowe Art Gallery and as a book reviewer for the *Miami Herald*. At present, she is living in Chapel Hill, North Carolina. *The Jew Store* received starred reviews from *Kirkus Reviews* and from *Booklist*, the publication of the National Library Association. Kirkus said of the book that it was "An admirable debut . . . vividly told and captivating in its humanity," and *Booklist* called it "An absolute pleasure." Stella Suberman is also the author of *When It Was Our War: A Soldier's Wife on the Homefront* (Algonquin Books, 2003), which was a 2004 SEBA Book Award Nominee in Nonfiction and which received a starred review and the designation of "Editor's Pick" from *Publishers Weekly*. The third book of her memoir trilogy, titled *"G.I.'s and the Bill That Empowered America: A Memoir,"* awaits publication.

BARBARA BROWN TAYLOR teaches religion at Piedmont College in rural northeast Georgia and is an adjunct professor of spirituality at Columbia Theological Seminary. An Episcopal priest since 1984, she is the author of twelve books, including the *New York Times* bestseller *An Altar in the World*, published by HarperOne in February 2009. Her first memoir, *Leaving Church*, which tells the story of her decision to leave parish ministry for classroom teaching, won a 2006 Author of the Year award from the Georgia Writers Association. As the *Sewanee Theological Review* has noted, Taylor "possesses a gift that is in short supply these days: the gift of conveying a living sense of the transcendent, the holy, and the grace-full in and through the stuff of our lives." She and her husband, Ed, live on a working farm in the foothills of the Appalachians with wild turkeys, red foxes, two old quarter horses, and far too many chickens.

ALICE WALKER is a prolific writer in multiple genres. Walker published her debut novel, *The Third Life of Grange Copeland*, in 1970, followed by *Meridian* (1976). In 1982, Walker published *The Color Purple*. For this achievement, Walker was awarded the 1983 Pulitzer Prize for Fiction (the first African American woman writer to receive this award) and the American Book Award. Walker has published four other novels, several volumes of poetry, four collections of short stories, and six volumes of nonfiction prose, including *In Search of Our Mothers' Gardens* (1983). Walker has been writer-in-residence at Mississippi's Jackson State University and Tougaloo College and has taught at the University of Massachusetts at Boston and Wellesley College. Walker also served as an editor at *Ms.* magazine and, in 1984, established Wild Trees Press. Walker's writings have been translated into more than two dozen languages, and her books have sold more than ten million copies. Along with the Pulitzer Prize and the American Book Award, Walker's awards and fellowships include a Guggenheim Fellowship and a residency at Yaddo. In 2006, Walker was honored as one of the inaugural inductees into the California Hall of Fame. In 2007, Walker appointed Emory University as the custodian of her archive, which opened to researchers and the public on April 24, 2009.

CIA WHITE teaches high school English and Creative Writing in Louisville, Kentucky.

Permissions